Save $1000 In 90 Days Challenge

Dexter L. Jones

Save $1000 In 90 Days Challenge

Uwriteit Publishing Company, Goldsboro, NC 27530

www.theuwriteitpublishingcompany.weebly.com
www.save1000dollarsin90days.com
www.dexterljones.com

ISBN-13: **978-1496032263**
ISBN-10: **1496032268**

First Printing — July 2014

This publication is designed to provide information in regard to the subject matter covered. It is published with the understanding that the author is not engaged in rendering legal counsel or other professional services. If legal advice or other professional advice is required, the services of a professional person should be sought.

Printed in the U.S.A.

DEDICATION

I would like to dedicate this book to all those who were partakers of the first 90 Day Challenge in the month of February 17, 2014- May 17, 2014. Also, to all those that will partake of this 90 Day Challenges, this book is for you.

INTRODUCTION

Welcome to the **"Save $1000 in 90-Days Challenge."** This is the book where you will learn how to save $1000 in the next 90-Days on a continuous basis. Get ready for the one book that is on a mission to put money in your pocket.

If you're ready to change your financial situation and learn how to save $1000 in the next 90 Days then this book is for you. We're not asking anyone to spend additional money during these 90 days, but we will give you daily tips and suggestions to make it happen. If you're up for the challenge then get on board.

If you want financial stability in your life then you're going to have to change the very core of your being. What is in you right now is not what you need to see the financial changes in your life. If you want to see your financial life explode then you must begin to do something different than what you're currently doing! You will have to make a change in your thinking, in your habits, in your actions and in your talking.

Do not allow this year financially to be like last year and years gone by. You must begin anew. Someone said, *"I wish there was some wonderful place called the Land of Beginning Again."* Well, there is such a place and it is in your own heart and mind. You are where you are today because of the thoughts, habits and actions that are dominating your mind and spirit.

In order to change your situation you must have access to new thoughts, new habits, new talking and new actions! We are on a mission to show you how to get into a financial realm in life that will change everything around you. God wants you to prosper. The word of God says, *"Beloved, I wish above all things that thou mayest prosper and be in health, even as thy soul **prospereth**."* 3 John 1:2 The question is do you want to prosper? If your answer is yes, then let's begin ANEW NOW!

Where Are You Today?

1. How much money did you save last year? _____

2. How much money did you save the year before? _____

3. How much money do you have in your savings now? _____

4. Would you like to have $1000 in your savings Yes___ No___?

Well, I can show you how to make that happen.

This Challenge can and will bring you out. Within this book are the greatest financial increase strategies, tips, ideas, concepts and principles you will ever come across. What I want you to commit to from this day forward is to pay the price in application to do what this book tells you, so that you can get from where you are to where you desire to be.

The greatest principles in the world will not work unless they are applied. You are about to learn infallible and time honored principles that will give you financial increase as sure as the night follows the day, and these principles belong to you just as much as they belongs to anyone else.

This book consists of a 90 day challenge to get $1,000 in your savings account in the next 90 days. Within this book are laid out all the strategies, ideas, plans, concepts, methods and principles to make this happen for you!

Make a commitment to yourself that you will apply these time honored principles that will put $1,000 in your account within the next 90 days. Here is a commitment declaration that you can commit to in order to change your financial situation. God Bless You!!

"I _____, commit to applying these time honored and tested principles in my life. I will give my all to the application of these strategies, tips, ideas and principles so that I can start my journey to financial increase. If it's to be, it's up to me"

Date: _____

Signature: _____

Save $1000 In 90 Days Challenge

The first thing that I will ask you to do today is to start off the Challenge by going in your purse, wallet or wherever you keep your money and get out a bill ($1, $5, $10, $20, $50 or $100) of any denomination (if you have no bills then you can gather together at least a dollars worth of change) to start off the challenge with.

Now the challenge begins and you are less that amount from reaching your $1000 goal in 90 days. (Example, if the amount you start with is $1, then you are $999 away from your $1000 goal). If you are married you can get your spouse to participate and the two of you can take the Challenge together for the next 90-Days or you can do it separately.

If this is something that you personally don't need but you know someone that's having financial problems (maybe your child, a friend, a neighbor, etc…) then purchase this book for them. This will be a 90-Day Challenge to help them get their finances on the right track. It will be a true blessing for them and they will be better off financially 90 days from now.

LET THE CHALLENGE BEGIN!!!

Save $1000 In 90 Days Challenge

CONTENT

1. Day 1 Challenge & Conclusion

2. Day 2 Challenge & Conclusion

3. Day 3 Challenge & Conclusion

4. Day 4 Challenge & Conclusion

5. Day 5 Challenge & Conclusion

6. Day 6 Challenge & Conclusion

7. Day 7 Challenge & Conclusion

8. Day 8 Challenge & Conclusion

9. Day 9 Challenge & Conclusion

10. Day 10 Challenge

11. Day 11 Challenge & Conclusion

12. Day 12 Challenge & Conclusion

13. Day 13 Challenge & Conclusion

14. Day 14 Challenge & Conclusion

15. Day 15 Challenge & Conclusion

16. Day 16 Challenge & Conclusion

17. Day 17 Challenge & Conclusion

18. Day 18 Challenge & Conclusion

19. Day 19 Challenge & Conclusion

20. Day 20 Challenge & Conclusion

21. Day 21 Challenge & Conclusion

22. Day 22 Challenge & Conclusion

23. Day 23 Challenge & Conclusion

24. Day 24 Challenge & Conclusion

25. Day 25 Challenge & Conclusion

26. Day 26 Challenge & Conclusion

27. Day 27 Challenge & Conclusion

28. Day 28 Challenge & Conclusion

29. Day 29 Challenge & Conclusion

30. Day 30 Challenge & Conclusion

31. Day 31 Challenge & Conclusion

32. Day 32 Challenge & Conclusion

33. Day 33 Challenge & Conclusion

34. Day 34 Challenge & Conclusion

35. Day 35 Challenge & Conclusion

36. Day 36 Challenge

37. Day 37 Challenge

38. Day 38 Challenge & Conclusion

39. Day 39 Challenge

40. Day 40 Challenge & Conclusion

41. Day 41 Challenge

42. Day 42 Challenge & Conclusion

43. Day 43 Challenge & Conclusion

44. Day 44 Challenge

45. Day 45 Challenge & Conclusion

46. Day 46 Challenge & Conclusion

47. Day 47 Challenge & Conclusion

Save $1000 In 90 Days Challenge

48. Day 48 Challenge & Conclusion

49. Day 49 Challenge

50. Day 50 Challenge & Conclusion

51. Day 51 Challenge

52. Day 52 Challenge & Conclusion

53. Day 53 Challenge

54. Day 54 Challenge & Conclusion

55. Day 55 Challenge

56. Day 56 Challenge

57. Day 57 Challenge

58. Day 58 Challenge

59. Day 59 Challenge

60. Day 60 Challenge

61. Day 61 Challenge

62. Day 62 Challenge

63. Day 63 Challenge

64. Day 64 Challenge

65. Day 65 Challenge

66. Day 66 Challenge

67. Day 67 Challenge

68. Day 68 Challenge

69. Day 69 Challenge

70. Day 70 Challenge

71. Day 71 Challenge

72. Day 72 Challenge

73. Day 73 Challenge

74. Day 74 Challenge

75. Day 75 Challenge

76. Day 76 Challenge

77. Day 77 Challenge

78. Day 78 Challenge

79. Day 79 Challenge

Save $1000 In 90 Days Challenge

80. Day 80 Challenge

81. Day 81 Challenge

82. Day 82 Challenge

83. Day 83 Challenge

84. Day 84 Challenge

85. Day 85 Challenge

86. Day 86 Challenge

87. Day 87 Challenge

88. Day 88 Challenge

89. Day 89 Challenge

90. Day 90 Challenge

SAVE $1000 IN 90 DAYS CHALLENGE

Chapter 1

Day 1 CHALLENGE & CONCLUSION

Good Morning and welcome to **the "Save $1000 in 90-Days Challenge."** Are you ready for your first day of challenge to help you save $1000 in the next 90 Days?

TODAY'S WORDS

Usually saving for the future means a sacrifice in the here and now. This can make saving feel like a chore, and no one likes a chore. Therefore, to help smooth the process, choose something that you want to buy when you reach your $1000 goal that will cost you maybe 10-20% of your goal (or that is $100-$200) as your reward for achieving your goal. This is the big picture to help keep you focused on your goal. Next, take a picture or cut out a picture and post it on your freezer or put a photo on your phone where you can see it daily for your motivation. (For example, my photo will be of a new suit that I want to buy).

The number 1 reason that people aren't able to save is because they have no plan. And if you fail to plan then you plan to fail. This means that if you're not planning to succeed financially, then you're planning to fail financially.

FIRST THING FIRST

The first thing you must learn to do is TRACK YOUR SPENDING! People spend between $3-$10 a day (some more) on breakfast, lunch and during break time (at work), starting today take notice of this.

DAY 1--THE CHALLENGE

Don't spend your money during your break time at work.

Your challenge for today is to not spend money during your break times. The amount that you would normally spend during your break(s) take it home and put it in a jar, can or wherever you can put it away (we will call this jar, can, etc.., your $1000 Prosperity Bank). Note: You will not die if you don't eat during your break time (or lunch if you don't normally spend during break,) today but you will be that much closer to reaching your $1000 saving in 90-Days. Remember, it's not how much money you have or make that counts, its how much you save and how you manage it!

This is your challenge for today--DON'T SPEND YOUR MONEY DURING YOUR BREAK TIMES-BUT SAVE IT!

CONCLUSION

Greetings, I want to thank everyone for taking out the time to Challenge yourself today with the Day 1 Challenge of NOT SPENDING YOUR MONEY DURING YOUR BREAK TIMES-BUT SAVING IT! This is a challenge not only that you did today but you can do it daily or as often as you can to SAVE toward your $1000 Goal. Every time you save that break money it's adding up to your ACCOUNT (Think about it).

The word CHALLENGE means a call or

summons to engage in a fight or battle so as to make a demand on a cause. In this case your finances. Each day there will be a different challenge to engage in.

I hope that you have put aside your starting amount and also the photo of the reward you will get at the end of the challenge. Those of you that did not put your money and photo aside I encourage you to do it now because the doing gives you vision and call you to action. *For where there is no vision the people perish (perish means to cast off restraint and do anything). Proverbs 29:18* So let's cast vision on today and eradicate procrastination right away. Many of these challenges will call you to take action by doing something.

Remember every dollar saved gets you closer to your goal and faith without works is dead. James 2:20 As you persist daily the financial change is happening and within 90 Days with God's help it shall happen. Also during these 90-Days let's believe God for financial miracles along with our actions as you partake of these challenges.

In closing have a great night and keep a mindset of expectation and anticipation, daily visualizing your goal as already reached and seeing yourself in possession of $1000. Talk with you tomorrow with another great challenge.

Chapter 2

Day 2 CHALLENGE & CONCLUSION

God bless you and good morning, welcome to Day 2 of **the "Save $1000 in 90-Days Challenge."** Are you ready for your second day of challenge to help you save $1000 in the next 90 Days?

TODAY'S WORD

TAKING THE TIME TO SET GOALS TODAY ALLOWS YOU TO ACHIEVE WHAT YOU WANT IN THE FUTURE. Without goals, purposes and plans are not accomplished. The majority of people have no financial goals therefore the majority of people never achieve their financial aim. A goal is an end toward which an effort is directed. It is an aim, mark, target, point or a clearly directed intent or purpose. Your goal for the next 90-Days is to save $1000, this is your mark and in order to reach it you must form new habits. Your old habits have not enabled you to save as you desire but your new habits will.

Successful people have the habit of doing things failures don't like to do. Because it is easier to continue with old habits and endure a life of poverty and barely making ends meet, than it is to change ourselves for a better life people will normally continue with old habits. But not you, today you throw off those old habits like a caterpillar sheds its skin, today is a new day for you and a time of financial growth has arrived. The caterpillar's "skin" or cuticle is like a shell - it does not grow. As the caterpillar body grows bigger and bigger, it outgrows its skin and needs to SHED it.

The caterpillar squeeeeezes, pushes and tugs as it wiggles out of its tight old skin. Then it rubs off its FACE MASK. Even the face mask has become too small. You are like that caterpillar, your old habits and way of thinking is to small for you now, for the next 90 days you will stretch yourself, squeeze, push, tug and wiggle your way out of your old financial ways and your new ways will equip you to save that $1000 in the next 89 days.

DAY 2-THE CHALLENGE

Save $1000 In 90 Days Challenge

Skip the Convenience Store.

Most people have a tendency to stop at a convenience store to pick up a little something not realizing that those nickels and dimes adds up to dollars and hundreds over time. A daily stop at a convenient store can add up to 2-3 dollars a day. That adds up to $60-$90 a month and if your spouse stops on their way home that's another $60-$90, now you're at $120-$180 a month and throw something in for the kids and you're easily at $150-$200 a month without even realizing it. For the next month plan ahead for your snacks away from home and put all that saved money toward your $1000 Challenge into your Prosperity Fund Account.

CHALLENGE FOR TODAY

Skip the convenience stores for the next month and begin to plan ahead for what you need--shed that old habit of making the convenience stores prosperous and add to your $1000 goal.

CONCLUSION

Well, we come to the close of Day 2 of the "The Save $1000 in 90-Day Challenge," you have gone the extra mile today in taking up this challenge and you have been rewarded with extra money to put in your "$1000 Prosperity Bank."

Today was not an easy challenge but you rose to the challenge and you will reap the benefits and daily those benefits will continue to add up. As you continue to shed the old habits and create new ones you will find yourself achieving financial goals that you only once dreamed of. Continue to be like the caterpillar and squeeeeze, push, tug and wiggle your way to "Saving $1000 in 90-Days."

Even if you were not able to save anything today it doesn't stop your challenge but persist and persevere until the end and you will win. For a winner never quits and a quitter never wins.

Last night closing remarks I asked you all

to pray about financial miracles during this time for all those that are participating--well today I received in the mail a post card from a business that I had put some money down on a item over a year ago-- and the postcard said we have put the item back but you can come and pick up the refund. Folks this has been over a year ago and I haven't even thought about it. Of course some of this money is going in my "$1000 Prosperity Bank." Keep the faith and keep a mindset of expectation and anticipation, daily visualizing your goal as already reached and seeing yourself in possession of $1000. Talk with you tomorrow morning with another great challenge.

Chapter 3

Day 3 CHALLENGE & CONCLUSION

God bless you and good morning to a group of winners that has decided to take their financial future into their own hands to bring about a change. Welcome to Day 3 of the **"Save $1000 in 90-Days Challenge."** Are you ready for your third day of challenge to help you save $1000 in the next 90 Days?

TODAY'S WORD

The word for today is **CHANGE** and change is defined as: the act or instance of making or becoming different. As a participant of the "Save $1000 in 90-Day Challenge" you are on a mission to make a change in your financial situation, you're tired of doing business the same old way and you realize that "If you want something that you've never had, then you must do something that you've never done." For many this is a true challenge to begin to direct their money in a different way to create different results.

During this 90-Day duration you're not going to be a person that sit back and wait on LUCK but you will be a person that creates their own LUCK which is defined as Labor Under Correct Knowledge. Your financial prosperity can be predicted with 100% accuracy and during this duration with God's help that's what you will do. You are using your mind to plan your financial future and take charge of your money.

DAY 3 CHALLENGE

Save Your Change.

Most individuals spend money on a daily basis on something and when you spend that money the majority of the time you will get back some change. Your mission today and for the next 87-days is to save that change and put it away in your $1000 Prosperity Bank. There have been individuals that have saved hundreds and thousands of dollars in change alone. Each day you save that change you are increasing financially. *"For who hath despised the day of small things?" Zechariah 4:10* For small things will create a big CHANGE! *This is your challenge for today--save your change from this point on*!

CONCLUSION

Another Day of Victory for the Team, truly people is being impacted by the daily challenges and it's having an effect on their financial decisions. Here is a brief testimony from today: Shirley Howard: I stopped to the store last evening and this challenge was on my mind as I thought about each item that I purchased. I asked myself if I could do without or if I really needed it. This is great.

What we are experiencing is change-the act or instance of making or becoming different. You're making different decisions in your thinking, in your spending and you're focusing on the outcome of this 90 Day Challenge. This is a good thing and it's drawing you financially closer to reaching your goal of "Saving $1000 in 90 Days."

The challenge today called for you to "Save Your Change" from this day forward and put it in your $1000 Prosperity Bank. A young man told about how he was able to save $4000 by simply not spending his change, if he can do it you can do it.

This is your time and you now have more money in your savings than you had last week, but this is only the beginning, there are greater things to come. Small keys open big doors and you have received a different key everyday that will stretch your mind to a shape that it has not known before.

Keep the faith and keep a mindset of expectation and anticipation, daily visualizing your goal as already reached and seeing yourself in possession of $1000. Talk with you tomorrow morning with another great challenge.

Chapter 4

Day 4 CHALLENGE & CONCLUSION

God bless you and good morning. Welcome to Day 4 of the **"Save $1000 in 90-Days Challenge."** Are you ready for your fourth day of challenge to help you save $1000 in the next 90 Days?

TODAY'S WORD

In order to accomplish your Goal of Saving $1000 in the next 90 Days you must begin to think outside the box. The truth of the matter is most people already have within their possession the ability or the means to make and save that $1000. Thinking outside the box (also thinking out of the box or thinking beyond the box) is a metaphor that means to think differently, unconventionally, or from a new perspective.

It means approaching problems in new, innovative ways; conceptualizing problems differently; and understanding your position in relation to any particular situation in a way you'd never thought of before. We're told to "think outside the box" all the time, but how exactly do we do that? How do we develop the ability to confront problems in ways other than the ways we normally confront problems? How do we cultivate the ability to look at things differently from the way we typically look at things?

DAY 4 CHALLENGE

See if you can pick up some overtime on your job (business).

Our goal is to save $1000 in 90-Days. Here is a strategy to add to the bottom line that you may have not thought of or you may have simply boxed your thinking to simply your weekly routine.

If your job permits, see about an extra shift, working on a special project, filling in for someone who needs time off, or even become a temp, etc..., it may feel like you're putting in a lot of work, but remember this is only temporary to help your reach your goal of saving $1000 in 90-Days.

One day a week could enable you to reach your goal or put a substantial amount in your $1000 Prosperity Bank. Look at these figures. If you could work 1 extra shift or 8 hours a week. Let's say you're making $8.00 an hour. $8.00 x 8 hrs = $64 a week x 4 weeks a month = $256 x 3 months = $768.

If your job permits, go for it temporarily and your bank account will thank you at the end of 90-Days. Now this money that you make weekly or monthly is not to be spent but put in your $1000 Prosperity Bank to bring you closer to your desired goal.

DAY 4 CHALLENGE

Pick up some overtime on your job (business) or do some temp work once a week within the next 86 days.

CONCLUSION

Today the challenge asked you to think outside the box, because if you're going to change your situation you have to do something that you've never done. From this day forward you will be given challenges that will ask you to approach saving your $1000 through new, innovative ways. Ways you may have never thought of before. Not only that but we're going to not just think outside of the box but we're going to kick every box down and totally eradicate every box.

You are a winner and these 90 days are going to give you the opportunity to stretch yourself and see things from another perspective. $1000 in 90-Days is a great task to ask you to believe but if you can believe it you can achieve it. Some have not been able to save $1000 in years but through this 90-Day challenge you will achieve a feat that will be forever written in stone. The past is gone you cannot change it, the present is what you do in the now and the future is the time or a period of time following what you do in the moment. Today is your day to change history for you, your family and future generations to come.

The coming challenges will provoke your thinking and cause you to say WOW I didn't think about making and saving money this way. For the next 85 days it's on and as you will make it happen with God's help, no more guessing, hoping and wondering about saving, no, we will have a strategic plan and purpose to get you from where you started to where you want to be. Get ready to take on new ventures that will guarantee your success.

Keep the faith and keep a mindset of expectation and anticipation, daily visualizing your goal as already reached and seeing yourself in possession of $1000. Talk with you tomorrow morning with another great challenge.

Note: Also you can put in your $1000 Prosperity Bank any amount daily that you want to add on to your goal ($1, $5, $10, etc..), it all adds up!

Chapter 5

Day 5 Challenge & Conclusion

God bless you and good morning. Welcome to Day 5 of the **"Save $1000 in 90-Days Challenge."** Are you ready for your fifth day of challenge to help you save $1000 in the next 90 Days?

TODAY'S WORD

We have now entered Day 5 of the challenge and our first immediate goal is to save $100 by Day 10. This is definitely a possible goal to achieve if you have been following the challenges each day. However, no matter where you are on Day 10 you must not let up but continue to persevere. These challenges work if you will work them, you must become passionate and even diligent in your pursuit if you want to see this happen. Laziness and slothfulness will bring you to nothing. The Bible says: *"He also that is slothful in his work is brother to him that is a great waster. (But) the hand of the diligent maketh rich." Proverbs 18:9, 10:4*

DAY 5 CHALLENGE

Pay yourself when you get paid 10% and put it in your $1000 prosperity bank.

The challenge for today is to PAY YOURSELF. Many people get paid today and the first thing they will do is begin to separate their money to pay their bills. Most people never pay themselves anything. Listen to these questions.

- Why is it that some individuals get ahead well in life while others deal with living paycheck to paycheck?
- Why is it that some people can attract money while others barely make ends meet?
- Why is it that some people seem to be like a money magnet while others can't seem to get money to come to them no matter what?

The answer is the former have learned the principle of PAYING THEMSELVES. A tenth of what you make belongs to you. You must realize this here and now and make up your mind to appropriate this into your life. If you fail to do this all you're doing is working for others and putting money in their pockets making them wealthy while your pockets go lacking. When you pay everyone but yourself you might as well be a slave working for a master and giving him your salary as soon as you make it.

Ex. If you make $300 a week then 10% of that will be $30. If you can't start with 10% then do 5% which will be $15. At the very least start with 2% or $6. If you don't get paid today then your next payday and your remaining paydays, pay yourself until the end of the 90 day challenge!

CONCLUSION

Well we come to the close of Day 5 of the "Save $1000 in 90-Days Challenge". The goal that we stipulated on today was that we will have $100 in 10 days. This will be the start of our 90-Day Goals. We have several different goals such as Immediate Goals, Intermediate (Middle Goals) and Long Range Goals. Here they are as stated below:

- Immediate Goal (10 Days) = $100
- Intermediate Goals (45 Days) = $300-$500
- Long Range Goals (90 Days) = $1000

Folks it is happening, individuals are seeing a difference in their thinking and in the increase of their finances. We're not talking about wishful thinking or just hoping or praying for a change, but for a real manifestation of that change appearing before your eyes. Here are some of the things that the team members are saying:

- *My Change is making a CHANGE!!! YCM*
- *Thanks. I actually started saving before I was invited to this challenge. I had no goal. Thanks to you I do now! Look at God!! EBS*
- *I love this concept....I just put my "start" money in my challenge stash...90 day challenge...I love it...We can easily spend $1000 in minutes.... GR*

People this is truly amazing, it is happening and it will continue to happen as you follow the daily challenges that you can partake of. There are more that can go up here but these are just a few.

I challenged you today with the Day 5 Challenge to: PAY YOURSELF FIRST, this will be a huge addition to your $1000 goal and you must take massive action with this challenge on your pay days. Save a maximum of 10% or a minimum of 2%, JUST DO IT and you will be breaking free from the routine that has so long held you in financial bondage, financial stagnation and financial suicide. This is your chance to make it happen and it will happen for you in the next 85 days!

Keep the faith and keep a mindset of expectation and anticipation, daily visualizing your goal as already reached and seeing yourself in possession of $1000. Talk with you tomorrow morning with another great challenge. *You are one day closer to $1000.*

Chapter 6

Day 6 CHALLENGE & CONCLUSION

God bless you and good morning. Welcome to Day 6 of the **"Save $1000 in 90-Days Challenge."** Are you ready for your sixth day of challenge to help you save $1000 in the next 90 Days?

TODAY'S WORD

People are looking for a quick fix and they would rather play the Lottery with a hope and a wish than take control of their financial future by using a strategy, idea, plan and concept. I am not saying playing the lottery is right or wrong but what I am saying is that you have no control over the way those numbers roll in, but you do have control of what goes into your $1000 Prosperity Bank on a daily, weekly and monthly basis.

Be the change that you want to see manifested in your finances. Don't dwell on your past failures or attempts to save. The past is just that a past, the past is defined as that which is gone by in time and no longer existing. The past is no longer current.

DAY 6 CHALLENGE

Do some ODD JOBS.

If you can't do any overtime work on your job try to find some odd jobs you can do in your neighborhood. Do yard work, clean houses, baby-sit, wash cars, mow lawns, pet sit, take on a paper route, participate in a focus group, become a house sitter, become an organizer-garages, basements, closets, cupboards and junk drawers for others, tutor, do handyman (woman) work, sell produce. It's only for 90-Days.

Challenge for today: find an odd job where you can make some extra cash and put it in your $1000 prosperity bank!

CONCLUSION

Down 6 Days on the "Save $1000 in 90 days

Challenges" You are one day closer to achieving your goal and each day you are adding to your "Prosperity Bank."

This $1000 will renew your mind set and enlighten you to know that if you achieved this goal, with the right information, ideas, strategies and tips you can achieve any financial goal. Today we encouraged you in the morning word to forget the past because the past is no longer in existence; it is the present and the future that you want to focus on now. The present is the period of time now occurring and what you do NOW will set the tone for that which will happen at a later time.

The challenge for today encourages you to DO SOME ODD JOBS so that you can create some additional income for your 90-Day Challenge. These things can only add to your bottom line and in this 90 Day Challenge that's what it's all about. The challenges that I challenge you to do I do also and it is daily adding to my bottom line. This challenge is about change in your financial life. You were created to prosper in life and God wants you to excel in your finances.

In closing keep the faith and keep a mindset of expectation and anticipation, daily visualizing your goal as already reached and seeing yourself in possession of $1000. Talk with you tomorrow morning with another great challenge.

NOTE: You are one day closer to $1000 and you are leaving your past behind you.

Chapter 7

Day 7 CHALLENGE & CONCLUSION

God bless you and good morning. Welcome to Day 7 of the **"Save $1000 in 90-Days Challenge."** Are you ready for your seventh day of challenge to help you save $1000 in the next 90 Days?

TODAY'S WORD

Can you believe that we are already 1 week into our "Save $1000 in 90-Days Challenge." Many of you started out with High Hopes and Great Expectations in this challenge, well we have now come to Day 7 and I pray that your hopes and expectations are still great and that you are still resolute and determined to reach your goal. In life nothing is easy but all things are possible and in order to achieve anything it's going to take hard work and smart planning.

Nothing will just fall out of the sky but if you will plan for a successful future and you work that plan it will surely come to pass. All the money that you need to reach your goal is in the hands of other men (women), these daily challenges gives you the ideas, tips, strategies and concepts about how to get it out of their hands. You have to take the action to make it happen.

DAY 7 CHALLENGE

Do you know someone that owes you money?

Well these 90-days are the time to collect it, but you're going to collect it in a way that's going to be a win-win situation for both parties. Now, if someone has owed you money for a while then either they don't have the money to pay you or they are not thinking about paying you. So you have to do like the collection agency do, cut their bill in half and offer them a better opportunity to pay you.

Example: Let's say someone owes you $100, what you will do is go to them and say, "*I understand that it's been hard to repay me what you owe me, so if we can solve this pro-*

blem by me cutting this in half for you and call it even, let's do it and go forward."

So they can pay you an outright $50 or $25 for the next 2 weeks or even $10 for the next 5 weeks. The bottom line, this is money in your "Prosperity Bank" that you would have never gotten but now you will receive it through proper planning and strategy.
NOTE: This strategy came from AJ Jones.

CONCLUSION

Down 7 Days on the "Save $1000 in 90-Day Challenges." We have now ended 1 week of progress and prosperity. If you have been consistent with the challenge then you are further along financially with your savings today than you were a week ago.

TONIGHT'S WORD

As we go through each daily challenge you will notice that we have many different challenges that can add to the bottom line. Even though you may think that some of these challenges may not directly fit you the majority of them will.

The challenge for today was about wisely getting back the money that is owed you. Whether you get it back in one lump sum or over a period of time it's money in the bank. Many of these challenges you will be able to do on a continuous basis, they're not a one time event but a continuous and repeated effort. Here are the challenges that we've had during the first week:

1. **Day 1--Don't spend money during your break time.**
2. **Day 2--Skip the convenience stores.**
3. **Day 3--Save your change.**
4. **Day 4--Pick up some overtime on your job.**
5. **Day 5--Pay yourself first.**
6. **Day 6--Do some odd jobs.**
7. **Day 7--Get back money owed you.**

This is a list of our first week challenges. Continue to apply these challenges daily, weekly and monthly until the 90-Day Challenge is over and your bottom line will be $1000 in your Prosperity Bank. If you need to go back and see the challenges you can go to the "Announcing the Save $1000 in 90-Days Challenge" Page.

In closing keep the faith and keep a mindset of expectation and anticipation, daily visualizing your goal as already reached and seeing yourself in possession of $1000. Talk with you tomorrow morning with another great challenge.

NOTE: Make sure you check in on the challenge tomorrow, it's going to be AN amazing challenge that can add to the bottom line of some of the team members! This challenge may even get the $1000 in one lump sum!!!

SAVE $1000 IN 90 DAYS CHALLENGE

Chapter 8

Day 8 CHALLENGE & CONCLUSION

God bless you and good morning. Welcome to Day 8 of the **"Save $1000 in 90-Days Challenge."** Are you ready for your eighth day of challenge to help you save $1000 in the next 90 Days? This may be a little long, but it is worth it today!

TODAY'S WORD

Do you know the reality of making things happen vs. waiting for things to happen? This challenge is for people of ACTION not people who wait for things to happen. Each day I give you a challenge to pursue and unless you actively participate it will not happen, but if you put it into ACTION only then are you exercising FAITH. For faith without works (action) is dead, meaning no faith at all. The greatest challenges means nothing if they're not appropriated do them and you will see the manifestation before your eyes. Today I will give you one secret that I came across that many know nothing about, but my desire is to help you reach your goal of $1000 in 90 days.

DAY 8 CHALLENGE

Unclaimed assets / Free money

This is a challenge that you may find hard to believe that such things exist but exist they do. And many individuals have received $50, $100, $1000's of Dollars with this tip along. I am personally a recipient of UNCLAIMED ASSETS / FREE MONEY. Do you know there is actually FREE MONEY OUT THERE FOR YOU. This is no wishful thinking, no gimmicks; this is true, accurate facts.

Many times we assume that we know what we have coming to us and we have not overlooked any money that is due us. Well, how wrong I was, I didn't know that out there was due me UNCLAIMED MONEY that I knew nothing about. What was due me was $71.00 from my utility YEARS AGO and I found it in less than a minute through the information you will receive today.

There are many sources of UNCLAIMED MONEY that is waiting for you. There are billions of dollars available in free money sources. Sources that owe you money such as:

- Safe deposit boxes
- Stocks, bonds, mutual funds, dividends,
- Trust funds,
- Insurance policies,
- Utilities deposits,
- Escrow accounts
- Un-cashed checks and wages
- And much more....

Truly, this is information that many don't want you to know. Could you imagine how surprise I was when I found out that I had $71 in UNCLAIMED MONEY / FREE MONEY THAT WAS DUE ME FOR YEARS GONE BY. Well, here is the information and how to claim your money. Go to: http://www.missingmoney.com/ and put in your name and the state you live in or try other states you lived in and see what kind of money is due you. In some cases it even tells you a little about the amount. If you don't have any due you, try the names of your relatives and if you find money for them, work out a agreement with them to see if they will give you something for finding them money they didn't know they had. It all adds to the bottom line, money in your Prosperity Bank. Also, on this website you will see different areas they visit to give individuals an opportunity to find their money face to face at one of their local events. If you can't find it there scroll down on the page and click on where it says (Can't Find It?) ENJOY THIS!

CONCLUSION

Down 8 Days on the "Save $1000 in 90-Day Challenges." I hope the challenge for today was exciting and challenging for you and if you were able to find profit on that challenge by all means drop us a line to let us know. We're having great reviews from the challenge and we ask for your continual feedback in the days ahead. Take time to ask yourself how would your financial status have been if you would have began this challenge 10 or 20 years ago, imagine the financial status you would have today. If you could have done this challenge every 90 days, which would result to $4000 a year in savings, in 10 years you would have $40,000. In 20 years you would have $80,000 in your Prosperity Bank (and that's not including interest).

Well, we can't go back but we can start as one of our team members are doing now by starting their children on the 90 Day challenge so that they can reap the rewards in their childhood that we failed to reap. So why not get your child started on the "Save $1000 in 90-Days Challenge." They don't have to save a $1000 but even if they can simply save a $100, what rewards and benefits would that add up to in the coming years? Keep up the good work!

In closing keep the faith and keep a mindset of expectation and anticipation, daily visualizing your goal as already reached and seeing yourself in possession of $1000. Talk with you tomorrow morning with another great challenge.

Chapter 9

Day 9 CHALLENGE & CONCLUSION

God bless you and good morning. Welcome to Day 9 of the **"Save $1000 in 90-Days Challenge."** Are you ready for your ninth day of challenge to help you save $1000 in the next 90 Days?

TODAY'S WORD

The Bible says, *"Better is the end of a thing than the beginning thereof: and the patient in spirit is better than the proud in spirit."* *Ecclesiastes 7:8* When you are going forth to achieve a goal it's not how you start but it's how you end. The start may be rocky but if you will continue to the end the result will be great and along the way it's going to take patience and humility to achieve your pursuit. So hang in there and you will be glad you did in the end.

TODAY'S CHALLENGE

Have a yard sale.

Here is the opportunity to make a lot of money with one sweep, having your very own yard sale. This is something that practically everyone can do and it can bring in some great income. As the old saying goes, *"One man's trash is another man's treasure."* In other words somebody wants what you have in your house now. Here are some things to think about.

- **How many old clothes do you have that you haven't worn in years?**
- **How many things haven't you used in years?**
- **How many baby clothes and toys do you have at your house and your babies are now older?**
- **How much stuff are you just holding on to?**

All these things could be money in your Prosperity Bank! If you start today planning for your yard sale this weekend that's extra money toward your goal. It could be an extra, $100 - $1000 this weekend.

DAY 9 CHALLENGE

Have a yard sale this weekend or later.

CONCLUSION

Down 9 Days on the *"Save $1000 in 90-Day Challenges."*We're making continual progress as each of us applies the challenges to our daily lives.

TONIGHT'S WORD

I hope that the challenge on today got you to thinking about what you need to do this weekend and how you can possibly even make that $1000 this weekend. It has been done many times. What you need to know is that this 90 day challenge is not something that you have to think up every day to do, I am doing the thinking for you but I cannot do the ACTION for you. You must apply these awesome challenges in order to make it happen.

Remember why you started this challenge and the zeal and desire you had that first day. Well, renew that zeal and take up that torch once again because fulfilling this challenge will not only change your financial life but it can change the lives of generations to come. Many times people begin a thing but they don't finish and therefore they acquire an attitude of quitting and they find themselves giving up on many things in life and then begin to wonder why life is not fair. Life is fair but it does not have any pity on a quitter. That reminds me of a poem that I read years ago entitled:

I Bargained With Life for A Penny

I bargain with life for a penny.
And life would pay no more
However I begged at evening
When I counted my scanty store.

For life is a just employer
He gives you what you ask.
But once you have set the wages,
Why you must bear the task.

I worked for a menial's hire.
Only to learn dismayed,
That any wage I had asked of life
Life would have willingly paid.

In closing keep the faith and keep a mindset of expectation and anticipation, daily visualizing your goal as already reached and seeing yourself in possession of $1000. Talk with you tomorrow morning with another great challenge.

Chapter 10

Day 10 CHALLENGE

God bless you and good morning. Welcome to Day 10 of the **"Save $1000 in 90-Days Challenge."** Are you ready for your tenth day of challenge to help you save $1000 in the next 90 Days?

TODAY'S WORD

You are closer to your desired goal and further from where you been. Your involvement in this 90 day challenge shows that you are a person that's ready for a change or ready for even greater improvement. Through faith you are already at your goal and all daily actions that you take simply bring you closer to the actual manifestation of that goal. The person that's not achieving new financial goals is the person that is financially bankrupt already. As a part of this team you are an achiever and a financial winner that has chosen to change your situation for the better.

DAY 10 CHALLENGE

Open a checking or savings account for your prosperity account.

Take the money that you've saved these 10 days and open up a checking or savings account with the money that you have saved in this 90 day challenge.

Chapter 11

Day 11 CHALLENGE & CONCLUSION

God bless you and good morning. Welcome to Day 11 of the **"Save $1000 in 90-Days Challenge."** Are you ready for your eleventh day of challenge to help you save $1000 in the next 90 Days?

TODAY'S WORD

How important is this 90 day challenge? Well the other night as I was watching the news they begin to talk about how families and individuals need to learn how to save money. They went on to state that this is so vital in this day and time because of the economy and that individuals first goal should be to save $1000 as Emergency Money. Well team that tell us and confirms that we're on the right track and taking the right on course with the overall feel of society. Therefore this challenge is not just another good idea but it's really a God idea letting us know that it's time to position ourselves for financial change.

However only those that obey will reap the benefits, the Bible states "if ye be willing and obedient, ye shall eat the good of the land." Isaiah 1:19 So if you want the good of the land then it's going to take both obedience, work and willingness, the three things that most people shy away from.

I heard someone state that "Getting wealth is easy" well I disagree because if it was that easy then more would have it. It takes information, inspiration, dedication, application, motivation, concentration, activation, duplication and revelation to change your situation. It will not just happen you must take action to make it happen!

DAY 11 CHALLENGE

Sell some of your old gold:

How many of us have old gold laying around that we haven't worn in years and probably will never wear again? Well that's MONEY that you have laying around that could now be in your "Prosperity Bank."

Save $1000 In 90 Days Challenge

Like the challenge we talked about earlier this week, some people have old clothes and other items that could be sold at a yard sell and put money in their pocket, well this one is the same. However, you want sell it at a yard sell but some good places are:

- Jewelry shops
- Gold parties--It's just like a Tupperware party, but instead of going home with plastic and a hole in your wallet, you sell your gold and take home cash
- Pawnshops
- Mail away operations--the legitimate ones
- These are just a few of the ways to get that old gold out of your house into the right person's hand so that it can put money in your pocket.

CHALLENGE FOR TODAY: SELL YOUR OLD GOLD

CONCLUSION

Down 11 Days on the "Save $1000 in 90-Day

Challenge." When you look at your "Prosperity Bank" at eleven days what do you see? **Savings that you never had before.**

TONIGHT'S WORD

We are 11 days into the greatest financial challenge of your life that will make all the difference in your financial portfolio. If you will stick with this until the end your financial outlook and mindset will never be the same. At the end you will know that all things truly are possible and no one will ever be able to tell you again that you can't change your financial situation.

You will know that truly there is a science to saving and savings comes not to the lazy, indolent, shiftless and do-nothing crowd, but to the diligent, persistent, industrious and hard-working crowd. Saving gets no easier than this 90 day challenge because here you're being instructed and given ideas about how to save.

If you need additional MOTIVATION make up a sign that you can put up around your house that says "Save $1000 in 90-Days Challenge" so that you can constantly see it daily as motivation.

In closing keep the faith and keep a mindset of expectation and anticipation, daily visualizing your goal as already reached and seeing yourself in possession of $1000. Talk with you tomorrow morning with another great challenge.

Chapter 12

DAY 12 CHALLENGE & CONCLUSION

God bless you and good morning. Welcome to Day 12 of the **"Save $1000 in 90-Days Challenge."** Are you ready for your twelfth day of challenge to help you save $1000 in the next 90 Days?

TODAY'S WORD

The difference between those that succeed and those that fail in life is one word, ACTION. This word is defined as: the fact or process of doing something, typically to achieve an aim. There are many that saw this challenge in the very beginning and knew that they needed a financial change but they still refused to take ACTION. They want something to drop out of the sky for them. Then there are those that started out but then stopped. The Bible says, "You did run well, who did hinder you?" Galatians 5:7 The truth is you hindered yourself. If you ever want to see a financial change then you must do something and do it over and over and over again until you achieve your aim.

DAY 12 CHALLENGE

Sell blood plasma.

This is a unique challenge that goes in a roundabout way to add to the bottom line but add to the bottom line it will. It is good to volunteer and give blood for FREE, but here is an opportunity for you to do it and make some money. Most places will pay you $20-$30 each time you visit to give plasma and you can do this twice a week. That comes to $40-$60 a week, $160-$240 a month, in 3 months time that equals $480-$720. If you can stand the NEEDLE then here's money waiting for you. Here is some information about selling blood plasma and locations. Here is even a video that tells more about it.

TALECRIS   =
http://www.talecrisplasma.com/html/index.htm

Save $1000 In 90 Days Challenge

BIOLIFE PLASMA CENTER =
https://www.biolifeplasma.com/index.html

BIOTEST PLASMA CENTER (FOR STUDENTS ONLY)
http://biotestplasma.com/

DCI BIOLOGICALS, INC
http://www.dciplasma.com/index.html

OCTAPHARMA PLASMA
http://www.octapharmaplasma.com/
VIDEO OF HOW TO GET PAID TO

DONATE PLASMA
http://www.youtube.com/watch?v=8yTYF5X69bY

CHALLENGE FOR TODAY: SELL BLOOD PLASMA

CONCLUSION

Down 12 Days on the "Save $1000 in 90-Day Challenge. Following these daily challenges that fit you and that you can apply will stretch you to new measures you've never encountered before.

TONIGHT'S WORD

The only thing that will stop you from obtaining your $1000 goal is if you lose your focus during these 90 days. A lack of focus is one of the major reasons why individuals don't achieve their financial goals. Focus is defined as: the state or quality of having or producing clear visual definition. Get clear and stay clear about what you want and you shall receive it. Mark 11:24

In closing keep the faith and keep a mindset of expectation and anticipation, daily visualizing your goal as already reached and seeing yourself in possession of $1000. Talk with you tomorrow morning with another great challenge.

Chapter 13

DAY 13 CHALLENGE & CONCLUSION

God bless you and good morning. Welcome to Day 13 of the **"Save $1000 in 90-Days Challenge."** Are you ready for your thirteenth day of challenge to help you save $1000 in the next 90 Days?

TODAY'S WORD

The actions you take today will determine your future tomorrow(s). If you do nothing today then nothing is set in motion for your future for nothing from nothing leaves nothing. One thing that will fight you along the way and cause you to procrastinate your financial future is your mind, so therefore you must renew your mind to catch up with YOUR financial desires. Romans 12:2. The mind will give you many reasons why you cannot achieve your $1000 financial goal such as:

- You've never done this before.
- This takes too much effort.

- You got to do something to make this happen (hello)
- I don't have the time.
- Who is going to help me do this?

Nothing but excuses and your reasons or explanation put forward to defend or justify your fault. Let's get rid of all excuses for achieving $1000 in 90 days, it's been done before and it will be done again and again and again, etc... While you make excuses somebody will be and is doing what you say can't be done.

DAY 13 CHALLENGE

Sell something on ebay.

Many individuals have made hundreds and thousands of dollars selling something on ebay. Selling stuff on ebay in my opinion is the modern day way of having a yard sale on line, but your customer base is so much bigger, the world gets to shop for your stuff. Stuff you no longer use and don't need. Just about everyone has something they can sell on ebay. First thing, get rid of all excuses about selling on ebay. Excuses such as:

- I don't have anything to sell.
- No one wants my stuff.
- I don't have time to learn how to sell stuff online.

Here's what you need to do, go to ebay and register to set up an account. Follow the instructions and start selling your stuff.

www.ebay.com

CHALLENGE FOR TODAY: sell something on ebay. Happy selling, you can even set it up right from your phone. Thank God for technology!

CONCLUSION

Down 13 Days on the "Save $1000 in 90-Day Challenge. A $1000 is just the starting point of a great saving program. If you can manage this the rest will be a piece of cake.

TONIGHT'S WORD

Save $1000 In 90 Days Challenge

Saving a $1000 is considered having an emergency fund in your possession so that when something comes up you have money that you can grab hold on to assist you out of that emergency. However, the sad reality is that most people don't have and can't get hold of that $1000 but through this challenge you will be one of the few that will have this in your possession from now on. This first 90 day challenge is just the beginning and it is something that you can continue to do to add on to your first saving of $1000. After this, look out world because your mindset and finances will never ever be the same again.

In closing keep the faith and keep a mindset of expectation and anticipation, daily visualizing your goal as already reached and seeing yourself in possession of $1000. Talk with you tomorrow morning with another great challenge.

CHAPTER 14

DAY 14 CHALLENGE & CONCLUSION

God bless you and good morning. Welcome to Day 14 of the **"Save $1000 in 90-Days Challenge."** Are you ready for your fourteenth day of challenge to help you save $1000 in the next 90 Days?

TODAY'S WORD

If you can save money today then you can save money tomorrow and the next day, etc... The key is to get into a habit of doing this. A habit is defined as a settled or regular tendency or practice, esp. one that is hard to give up. Your saving must become a habit in every sense of the word. These daily ideas, strategies, concepts are designed to show you how to save and make money and then save the money you make.

DAY 14 CHALLENGE

Become an independent consultant of some kind.

The task of a consultant is to provide advice to an individual or organization about matters in a specific niche.

- What do you know?
- What are you great at?
- What do you do that others just rave about?
- What could you teach others?

There are many that want to know what you know and will even pay you for what you know. During this 90 day challenge become a consultant and get paid for the consultation that you normally give for free.

CONCLUSION

Down 14 Days on the "Save $1000 in 90-Day Challenges." To many this challenge will be a wake-up call to give directions either to a financial portfolio that fell asleep years ago, or a benefit to a portfolio that's already thriving.

TONIGHT'S WORD

Every person that eventually woke up to the importance and necessity of money realized that if they will have money in their possession they must learn not to throw away their money on emotional buying, but learn to save their money so that their money can work for them instead of against them. Being broke is the pits because it limits what you can do and how you can do it. This 90 day challenge is designed to give you the first breakthrough in your finances that every financial teacher teaches you, which is to have in your possession EMERGENCY MONEY. When you have emergency money on hand then you don't have to borrow or use a credit card to pay for emergencies when they arise, because you will be financially fit to meet the emergencies.

In closing keep the faith and keep a mindset of expectation and anticipation, daily visualizing your goal as already reached and seeing yourself in possession of $1000. Talk with you tomorrow morning with another great challenge.

SAVE $1000 IN 90 DAYS CHALLENGE

CHAPTER 15

DAY 15 CHALLENGE & CONCLUSION

God bless you and good morning. Welcome to Day 15 of the **"Save $1000 in 90-Days Challenge."** Are you ready for your fifteenth day of challenge to help you save $1000 in the next 90 Days?

TODAY'S WORD

We're giving you all the tools you need to fulfill this challenge, your part is that you must commit to "Saving $1000 in 90 days." No one can make this commitment for you, it is personal and if it's to be it's up to you. The best laid out ideas, strategies, concepts and plans will not work (for you) if they're not applied. Application of those ideas, strategies, concepts and plans is the key to seeing change in your "Prosperity Bank." All of the challenges may not apply to you but the majority will and they will be enough to save $1000 in 90 days.

DAY 15 CHALLENGE

Pack lunch at least 3 times this week and put that money that you would normally spend in your prosperity bank.

This is a true challenge because many people go out to each lunch every day, not realizing the amount of money that they're spending on a weekly basis. I remember seeing individuals spending around $8-$10 a day at lunch time. With such spending you're talking about spending anywhere from $40-$50 a week and $160-$200 a month and $1920-$2400 a year. Money that could be going towards your savings!

CONCLUSION

Down 15 Days on the "Save $1000 in 90-Day Challenge." The commitment you make will open up a whole new avenue of consistency that will enable you to reach the financial goals that you so long for.

TONIGHT'S WORD

The challenge for today asks you to take a necessary action that will put you closer to achieving your $1000 goal. Every day this week that you bag that lunch you are doing something that those that want to save refuse to do, you are taking charge of your financial situation. Instead of putting money in the hands of the restaurants, fast food places or purchasing that $10 lunch you are preserving that money and the rewards at the end of the 90 days will speak for itself. This week you are helping yourself and God helps those that help themselves.

In closing keep the faith and keep a mindset of expectation and anticipation, daily visualizing your goal as already reached and seeing yourself in possession of $1000. Talk with you tomorrow morning with another great challenge.

Chapter 16

DAY 16 CHALLENGE & CONCLUSION

God bless you and good morning. Welcome to Day 16 of the **"Save $1000 in 90-Days Challenge."** Are you ready for your sixteenth day of challenge to help you save $1000 in the next 90 Days?

TODAY'S WORD

The desire to prosper and get ahead in life is a God given desire. It is not just a hope but it is one of God's highest desires for mankind. Poverty and lack is an enemy of both God and man, there is nothing good about it and the enemy not God glories in it. Therefore God says, *"Beloved, I wish above all things that thou mayest prosper and be in health, even as thy soul prospereth."* *3 John 1:2* There are no ifs, ands or buts about it God wants you to prosper. This 90 day challenge is designed to show you how to reach your first prosperous financial goal of saving $1000. God will not do it for you but he will grace your efforts as you put your faith into action!

DAY 16 CHALLENGE

Shop for grocery with a list.

When you go out to shop for grocery this week take a list of the items that you really need to purchase vs. just buying items when you shop. The number one cause of overspending during grocery shopping is IMPULSE BUYING.

Impulse buying is *Spur of the moment, unplanned decision to buy, made just before a purchase. Research findings suggest that emotions and feelings play a decisive role in purchasing, triggered by seeing the product or upon exposure to a well crafted promotional message. Such purchases ranges from small (chocolate, clothing, magazines) to substantially large (jewelry, vehicle, work of art) and usually (about 80 percent of the time) lead to problems such as financial difficulties, family disapproval, or feeling of guilt or disappointment.*

The key to avoiding unplanned purchases: SHOP WITH A LIST. You know what you normally spend each week when you shop, now with the money you will save for the next

90 days by shopping with a list, put that money in your "Prosperity Bank." Just another way to help you reach your goal of saving $1000 in 90 days.

Technology is a good thing and can help make your life easy, there is even an app that can assist you in your shopping and also let you know about deals of things you normally buy when they go on sale. Go to ZipList on your Smartphone.

Challenge for today: start using a list when you shop. Its money in your pocket and it stop you from impulse buying!

Chapter 17

DAY 17 CHALLENGE & CONCLUSION

God bless you and good morning. Welcome to Day 17 of the **"Save $1000 in 90-Days Challenge."** Are you ready for your seventeenth day of challenge to help you save $1000 in the next 90 Days?

TODAY'S WORD

Maybe some of you were not able to see any light at the end of your financial tunnel but if you've been following the challenges and saving then your light should be brighter than it was 17 days ago. According to statistics roughly three-quarters of Americans are living paycheck-to-paycheck, with little to no emergency savings.

Fewer than one in four Americans have enough money in their savings account to cover at least six months of expenses, enough to help cushion the blow of a job loss, medical emergency or some other unexpected event, according to the survey of

1,000 adults. Meanwhile, 50% of those surveyed have less than a three-month cushion and 27% had no savings at all.

That's why we're doing the 90 day challenge to show you how to save $1000 to help better equip you financially in life.

DAY 17 CHALLENGE

Shop at Dollar tree vs. Kroger, Harris teeter, etc… for some items.

Did you know that many of the very same items you purchase at KROGER, HARRIS TEETER, FOOD LION etc. you can purchase at Dollar Tree and save. I normally purchase my bread (among other items) at Dollar Tree because the same bread at other stores cost close to $3.00. With that in mind you are saving close to $2.00 on just this one item, that $2.00 now goes into my "Prosperity Bank." Take the time to go to a Dollar Tree and look at all the food items and other things you can purchase, the very same items those stores listed sell but at a higher price. Folks, this is about you not any love for those stores but about you and your family. You can easily walk out with a $10-$20 savings, that's money that goes toward your challenge and it could add up to hundreds in 90 days.

Challenge for today: visit dollar tree for some of the same items you purchase elsewhere. it's all about money in your pocket, not in their pocket!

CONCLUSION

Down 17 Days on the "Announcing the Save $1000 in 90-Day Challenge." The reality of individuals not having a substantial savings is real and those that refuse to change then there will be no change.

TONIGHT'S WORD

The importance of what we're facing as a people that lack savings is staggering. It is so amazing that I have to reiterate the statistics on today because this has to change.

In closing keep the faith and keep a mindset

of expectation and anticipation, daily visualizing your goal as already reached and seeing yourself in possession of $1000. Talk with you tomorrow morning with another great challenge.

Chapter 18

DAY 18 CHALLENGE & CONCLUSION

God bless you and good morning. Welcome to Day 18 of the **"Save $1000 in 90-Days Challenge."** Are you ready for your eighteenth day of challenge to help you save $1000 in the next 90 Days?

TODAY'S WORD

Financial literacy is necessary to stop living paycheck to paycheck! Culturally money is something that we don't discuss and therefore it's only something we talk about when it becomes a problem.

DAY 18 CHALLENGE

Use your iPhone to make money.

If you have a smartphone such as an iPhone, android, galaxy then you are a walking, talking cash register but you just don't know it yet. I have personally used my iPhone to make money doing things that I already do.

Save $1000 In 90 Days Challenge

There is a Revolution going on that consist of thousands of people that are changing their lives by simply using their iPhones to make money. You already have the iPhone now all you need to have is the information system in place to begin making money.

- How many times have you been to the grocery store this year or last year?
- What did you do with your receipts (if you're like most people you threw them away)?

Well, you threw away money that could have been in your account. But today you will learn how to put it in your Prosperity Account. If you have a smartphone on it you have either the App Store or the Play Store for downloading apps. Within that store is an app called RECEIPT HOG where you can SNAP YOUR RECEIPTS AND EARN CASH. Go to your app store and install this app and for every receipt you take a photo of and upload you earn coins that turns into actual cash in your account. I use this app often and it really works. Receipt Hog is a fun and rewarding way to turn receipts from everyday grocery shopping into cash - no matter where you shop or what you buy! You will simply need a Paypal account (which is free--just go to paypal.com to set it up) to receive your money.

CHALLENGE FOR TODAY: USE YOUR IPHONE TO MAKE MONEY!

TONIGHT'S WORD

The challenge for today was totally out of the box and way in left field, I bet you never heard of such a thing. A way to make money with the same device that you are walking around with daily. Never underestimate the ideas that you will come across in this 90 day challenge. We're here to WOW you, Challenge you, Provoke you and Empower you.

Well don't get relaxed because there is much more to come in the remaining 72 days that will forever change your financial status. There is money to be made in this world that will add to your bottom line and you will soon discover that it's awaiting your beckoning call.

In closing keep the faith and keep a mindset of expectation and anticipation, daily visualizing your goal as already reached and seeing yourself in possession of $1000. Talk with you tomorrow morning with another great challenge.

Chapter 19

DAY 19 CHALLENGE & CONCLUSION

God bless you and good morning. Welcome to Day 19 of the **"Save $1000 in 90-Days Challenge."** Are you ready for your nineteenth day of challenge to help you save $1000 in the next 90 Days?

TODAY'S WORD

If you want to truly succeed in this 90 day challenge then you must lay aside all slothfulness, laziness and being a sluggard. You must become an active diligent participant, one that is determined to make it happen.

I am reminded about the story in the Bible about the ant, it says; *"Go to the ant, thou sluggard; consider her ways, and be wise. Which having no guide, overseer, or ruler, Provideth her meat in the summer, and gathereth her food in the harvest (The ant has learned to store up, put aside and save). How long wilt thou sleep, O sluggard? when wilt thou arise out of thy sleep (when will you get up and do something)? Yet a little sleep, a little slumber, a little folding of the hands to sleep: So shall thy POVERTY come as one that travelleth, and thy WANT (poverty) as a armed man."* Proverbs 6:6-11

DAY 19 CHALLENGE

Sell some of the old stuff you have around the house on craigslist.

Here is another opportunity to sell some of the stuff you just have around that you're no longer using or have not used in years. This can turn into money in you PROSPERITY BANK. Somebody will be glad to have your old electronic gadgets, cell phones, etc... Some of you may have boxes that you've had packed up for years, get that stuff out of your hands and into somebody's hands that would be glad to have it.

Craigslist is a place that you can sell many different items. You may even have a car that you have been trying to sell; well Craigslist is the place to sell it. I have a brother that once sold a car on craigslist for over $2000. You can do the same--it's time to post your stuff on www.craigslist.com

CONCLUSION

Down 19 Days on the "Save $1000 in 90-Day Challenge." Do you want to be a part of the haves or the have-not?

TONIGHT'S WORD

In order to be a part of the haves then you must have. The first step to being a part of the haves is you must have $1000 in your savings; this $1000 is what is considered by many as EMERGENCY MONEY. When you have Emergency Money you no longer have to borrow or use a credit card to pay for emergencies because you have now entered the first phase of savings--$1000 IN YOUR POSSESSION. Keep up the good work and your Prosperity Bank will continue to grow daily.

In closing keep the faith and keep a mindset of expectation and anticipation, daily visualizing your goal as already reached and seeing yourself in possession of $1000. Talk with you tomorrow morning with another great challenge.

Chapter 20

DAY 20 CHALLENGE & CONCLUSION

God bless you and good morning. Welcome to Day 20 of the **"Save $1000 in 90-Days Challenge."** Are you ready for your twentieth day of challenge to help you save $1000 in the next 90 Days?

TODAY'S WORD

"Now Faith is the substance of things hoped for, the evidence of things not seen. Hebrews 11:1" This 90 day challenge is a challenge of faith not just belief, many believe they need a financial change but just to believe is not enough, because 90 days from our start date some that started out with us will not reach the goal. Not because they don't need it but because they didn't really want it bad enough to put ACTION behind their belief. To need something is one thing but to want it moves you from INACTION (PASSIVENESS) to ACTION (APPLYING THE CHALLENGES TO YOUR DAILY LIFE). Now this is FAITH.

DAY 20 CHALLENGE

Do online survey for extra cash.

Every dollar you make gets you closer to your goal so why not use some of your extra time while watching television, waiting in the checkout line, at the doctor's office, etc... to make you some extra cash. Taking surveys is one way to do this. It can bring you up to an extra $50 a month and that adds to your Prosperity Bank and your goal of $1000 in 90 days.

CHALLENGE FOR TODAY

Do online surveys for extra cash. and the cool thing about it is you can even do it from your Smartphone. Go to your app store and look for: MySurvey

But nevertheless here is the website: Paid Surveys - MySurvey - Online Surveys for Money, Take Survey
https://www.mysurvey.com

CONCLUSION

Down 20 Days on the "Save $1000 in 90-Day Challenge." Fear is faith in reverse and it takes you backwards instead of forward.

TONIGHT'S WORD

Each challenge is a test of your faith because either you will move forward, go backwards or remain the same. There is no way that you will go backwards or remain the same if you're applying these challenges to your life. If you are applying these tips, strategies and principles, go right now and look in your Prosperity Bank. What do you see on this 20th day? If you have been consistent you will see progress, prosperity, increase and more money in your SAVINGS than you saw 20 days ago. If you have not been consistent, then you will see stagnation, limitation, the same lack and deficiency.

If you want to get on prosperity side then from this day forward, change your mindset, change you actions and you will change your financial life. THIS IS WAITING FOR YOU!!

Chapter 21

DAY 21 CHALLENGE & CONCLUSION

God bless you and good morning. Welcome to Day 21 of the **"Save $1000 in 90-Days Challenge."** Are you ready for your twenty first day of challenge to help you save $1000 in the next 90 Days?

TODAY'S WORD

PERSISTENCE. Persistence is defined as firm or obstinate continuance in a course of action in spite of difficulty or opposition. During this 90 day challenge you will encounter some difficulty or opposition during your saving but you must continue is spite of it all. You have a goal to reach and your PERSISTENCE will get you there. Don't stop saving no matter what you encounter--put something in your Prosperity Bank daily and at the end your PERSISTENCE will help you to forge through every obstacle that stands between you and $1000.

DAY 21 CHALLENGE

Sell your old cell phone.

How many old cell phones do you have just laying around the house that you don't even use anymore? Those old cell phones could be money in your Prosperity Bank. Think you don't have anything to add to your savings, think again; just about everyone has old cell phones or know someone that does. It's time to dust them off and GET PAID!!! Here is the website that will show you what you need to do and they will get that check to you within 3 days (or through PayPal), WOW!

http://smartphonetradein.com/

CONCLUSION

Down 21 Days on the "Announcing the Save $1000 in 90-Day Challenge." Three weeks and counting not necessarily down, but up because financially you're further toward reaching your prosperity goal of saving $1000 in 90 days.

TONIGHT'S WORD

Three weeks in and it's going great. These challenge are working in the lives of many that are applying and taking advantage of this important information. You're getting these ideas, strategies, concepts and principles and they are tried and true. I want to see you reach this first goal of saving $1000 in 90 days.

Don't believe the lie that there isn't enough money in the world. According to my research so far I've seen that there is around 20 Trillion dollars in US money that exist in the world to date. Folks, that $20,000,000,000,000 so in other words somebody has your $1000, they may not give you $1000 in your hands but these challenges are telling you how to get, how to make it and how to save it. We have some good information coming, don't miss one day and apply the challenges that apply to you and don't just sit back and wait for something to happen, go and make something happen.

In closing keep the faith and keep a mindset of expectation and anticipation, daily visualizing your goal as already being reached and seeing yourself in possession of $1000. Talk with you tomorrow morning with another great challenge.

SAVE $1000 IN 90 DAYS CHALLENGE

Chapter 22

DAY 22 CHALLENGE & CONCLUSION

God bless you and good morning. Welcome to Day 22 of the **"Save $1000 in 90-Days Challenge."** Are you ready for your twenty second day of challenge to help you save $1000 in the next 90 Days?

TODAY'S WORD

PROGRESS. The word progress is defined as forward or onward movement toward a destination. Your destination is $1000 in your Prosperity Bank in 90 days and daily you're moving forward, onward with steady movement. Whatever you put in your savings today is progress and no matter how you look at it you're adding not subtracting from the bottom line.

On last night we talked about the amount of money in US currency and in my research the estimation was around 20 Trillion Dollars, that's 20,000,000,000,000 folks. Now somebody has your $1000 in their possession. How will you get it? Through making it and saving it. We have already given you 21 days of challenges that would cause you to have a good amount in your savings already. The question is what have you done with any of these challenges? Are you just opening up the book to read them daily or are you an active participant. If you're just reading them then you are just making motions but not progress and motions does not move you forward. So continue to make constant progress and not just motions.

DAY 22 CHALLENGE

Only shop with cash money this week.

When you go to the store and use your credit or debit card then you have a tendency to overspend and not stick to your budget. There is always a bargain that you seem to not be able to pass up and you end up spending more than you planned. Paying with a card is not like paying with real money because the card is not like actual money in your hands so it somewhat lose its value. But when you have cold hard cash in hand you don't spend so easily, you think twice and you consider your purchases. Now, you know what you normally spend each week in shopping, what you save by spending with CASH MONEY IN HAND; put that difference in your Prosperity Bank. That's more money added to your bottom line.

Chapter 23

DAY 23 CHALLENGE & CONCLUSION

God bless you and good morning. Welcome to Day 23 of the **"Save $1000 in 90-Days Challenge."** Are you ready for your twenty third day of challenge to help you save $1000 in the next 90 Days?

TODAY'S WORD

BIBLE. The word Bible is defined as the Christian scriptures, consisting of the 66 books of the Old and New Testaments. The Bible is the bestselling book of all time and there is a reason for that. The Bible is the book of life and it has all the answers for successful living and that includes how to save and make money. The Bible tells us the best role model for saving and how it's done. It says, *"Go to the ant."* *Proverbs 6:6a* God is giving us a directive and telling us the role model to go and learn about saving from, THE ANT.

Here is a tough truth to accept because many people don't like for you to tell them how to live, even if it's killing them physically or financially. To tell a person they need to change their eating habits and exercise or they will be dead in the next year is a tough pill to swallow. And some refuse to accept it. The reality is if you have no savings or you are a part of the 22% that has less than $100 in savings or part of the 46% that has less than $800, there is a reason why. According to the Bible the Ant is a very diligent, active, conscientious, persistent, steadfast, hard-working and unrelenting creature. But people that have no savings are just the opposite in their life when it comes to saving (not saying in all aspects of their life, but saving). They are lazy, careless, disinterested, ignorant, sluggard, inactive, thoughtless, slothful and negligent, when it comes to saving.

The Bible says, "*Go to the ant, thy sluggard; consider her ways, and be wise: Which having no guide, overseer, or ruler, Provideth her meat in the summer, and gathereth her food in the harvest. How long wilt thou sleep, O sluggard? when wilt thou arise out of thy sleep? Yet a little sleep, a little slumber, a little folding of the hands to sleep: So shall thy poverty come as one that travelleth, and thy want as an armed man (You can look forward to a dirt-poor life, poverty your permanent house guest!)."* *Proverbs 6:6-11* All this because the person is either ignorant about how to save, or they have refused the knowledge that they do know. However, with the 90 day challenge you will not have to be ignorant but you will have to apply what you know. Apply this knowledge and you will be blessed with $1000 in 90 days in your Prosperity Bank.

DAY 23 CHALLENGE

Put a bill of some denomination in your prosperity bank.

Doing this is challenging you to do what you would not have done today. It will take some faith to do this but it will add to your bottom line and get you that much closer to your bottom line of having $1000 in your possession in 90 days. See you on the other side of Victory!

Note: If you don't have a bill today, when you get one before this week is out put one in your Prosperity Bank.

CONCLUSION

Down 23 Days on the "Save $1000 in 90-Day Challenge." You have more this week than you had last week and next week you will have more than you have this week.

TONIGHT'S WORD

The lesson that will help you to get to the next level of $1000 in your Prosperity Bank is the word that was spoken on today. Four simple words--"*Go to the Ant.*" If you don't know what this means go back and read today's word and challenge. Also read Proverbs 6:6-11.

In closing keep the faith and keep a mindset of expectation and anticipation, daily visualizing your goal as already reached and seeing yourself in possession of $1000. Talk with you tomorrow morning with another great challenge.

Chapter 24

DAY 24 CHALLENGE & CONCLUSION

God bless you and good morning. Welcome to Day 24 of the **"Save $1000 in 90-Days Challenge."** Are you ready for your twenty fourth day of challenge to help you save $1000 in the next 90 Days?

TODAY'S WORD

If you want to get ahead financially in life then you must be diligent in your pursuit. Lazy people only get what's left behind and is always a day late and a dollar short. The Bible says, *"He becometh poor that dealeth with a slack hand: but the hand of the diligent maketh rich."* *Proverbs 10:4* What kind of hand do you have? Are you taking the initiative to save and apply these challenges or are you idle? A person that's spending time doing nothing, a person without purpose or effect; pointless. Yet you believe that your finances will just automatically turn around. Well, I repeat; *"He becometh poor that dealeth with a slack hand: but the hand of the diligent maketh rich."* *Proverbs 10:4*

DAY 24 CHALLENGE

Take your old items or things you no longer use or need and sell them at a flea market.

Here is a great way to make some extra cash for your Prosperity Bank. You will be amazed at what people will buy at a flea market. As the saying goes, one man's trash is another man's treasure. Somebody wants the stuff that you have laying around the house that you no longer use or need.

I was at a flea market this past week and next to me was a man that had boxes of stuff that you would think nobody wanted. Some of this stuff he really could have just taken to the dump, but lo and behold people were at his tables buying his stuff. I saw him sell one lady a box of stuff for $20 for the entire box and all day long they were buying his stuff. He was making $2 here, $5 here, $10 here, etc... If you will go on a weekend and sell your stuff you could probably leave with $100-$300 and that's money that will add to your bottom line of saving $1000 in 90 days. Will you put your hand to work and be diligent or will you allow your hand to be slack and let all that money you have in your house (in the form of stuff) just sit there while you say you have no money for savings?

CONCLUSION

Down 24 Days on the "Save $1000 in 90-Day Challenge." The journey of a thousand miles begins with one step.

TONIGHT'S WORD

Every step, every act that you take toward your $1000 challenge is getting you closer to the bottom line. The only ones that will not reach their goal are the ones that did not begin or the ones that began but quit before the end. And we all know that a winner never quits and a quitter never wins. **The $1000 is YOURS!**

Chapter 25

DAY 25 CHALLENGE & CONCLUSION

God bless you and good morning. Welcome to Day 25 of the **"Save $1000 in 90-Days Challenge."** Are you ready for your twenty fifth day of challenge to help you save $1000 in the next 90 Days?

TODAY'S WORD

Some things change and some things remain the same. In life there are some things that will never change. Two plus two will always be four. The end of every person is always death. Your race will never change and gravity will always pull you to the ground (Without any supernatural intervention from God these things will always remain the same). These things are considered absolutes. An absolute is something that is fixed, universal, decided and outright complete. It does not change and it will not change.

However your finances are not something

that is absolute, fixed, universal, complete and decided. The changing of your finances is dependent on what you do to produce a change. Therefore it is conditional, dependent, accountable and submissive to yield to how and which way you want it to go. You started on Day 1 with a certain amount, it is now day 25, the change in your finances to this day is dependent on what you have done to make the change. Because some things change and some things remain the same. The change is submissive and will yield to challenges which will simply add to the bottom line--money in your Prosperity Bank.

DAY 25 CHALLENGE

Cancel any memberships that you no longer use or only use here and there.

Why continue to pay a company for something that you don't use or rarely use, that's just money that you're throwing away monthly and that $30, $40, $50 or more is money that you could be putting in your Prosperity Bank. Stop filling these companies pockets by paying for something that you no longer use. FILL YOUR OWN POCKETS!

CONCLUSION

Down 25 Days on the "Save $1000 in 90-Day Challenge." People are destroyed for a lack of knowledge, but if you're a part of this 90-day challenge this does not include you. YOU'RE GETTING FINANCIAL KNOWLEDGE NOW!

TONIGHT'S WORD

People are saying and thinking that they have no money to save to reach their goal of saving $1000 in 90 days. But the truth of the matter is we do have money but we're wasting a lot of money that could be going into our saving or Prosperity Bank. Many times people are destroyed for a lack of knowledge or because they have rejected knowledge. Hosea 4:6

Our challenge for today talked about *cancelling any memberships that you no longer use or only use here and there and begin to put this money into your savings or prosperity bank.* During further research of this topic I have come to discover that 15% of Americans have a GYM MEMBERSHIP (this does not include other types of memberships). But only 8% of those who have memberships actually use them. WHAT A WASTE OF MONEY! Over half are not using them yet they're paying for the membership monthly.

This means that Americans are wasting $2.4 BILLION on gym memberships every year. The true reason for this waist in money is due to contracts and lack of motivation. STOP WASTING THIS MONEY AND START SAVING THIS MONEY. $2.4 Billion Dollars.

Chapter 26

DAY 26 CHALLENGE & CONCLUSION

God bless you and good morning. Welcome to Day 26 of the **"Save $1000 in 90-Days Challenge."** Are you ready for your twenty sixth day of challenge to help you save $1000 in the next 90 Days?

TODAY'S WORD

Don't rely on luck or a lucky break to get your finances to increase you must put forth the effort to make it happen. Beside's LUCK is simply Labor Under Correct Knowledge. Through this 90 day challenge you're getting the correct knowledge to change your situation and change it will. You're done with the days of waiting for success to be brought to you by chance rather than through one's own actions. In the course of these 90 days of challenge you're taking the initiative to apply what you're learning and make it happen. For God helps those that helps themselves, not those that sit on the side line and wait for something to happen.

Others will go pass them and the only thing they will be able to say at the end of these 90 days is WHAT HAPPENED, MY FINANCES ARE THE SAME!

DAY 26 CHALLENGE

Sell your old clothes at a consignment shop.

Do you have some old clothes around the house that you haven't worn in a while, then these clothes are great potential sells for the consignment shop. Do you have old baby clothes? Baby clothes and children clothes are great sellers and are greatly appreciated at consignment shops. So go through your closet and boxes and clean them up and go get your money to put in your Prosperity Bank. **YOUR MONEY WAITS!**

TONIGHT'S WORD

Many started the 90 day challenge with the utmost belief that this was the event that would create that financial change which they needed so much. But the truth of the matter is that your belief alone will not create the change because belief is simply an acceptance that a statement is true or that something exists. That is the simple truth and many accepted the challenge but only those that moved from belief to faith which is the act of putting action and works behind your acceptance, nothing will happen for the believers. Faith is acting on what you believe. If you want to save that $1000 in 90 days and go to the next level then you must take action and begin to act on these challenges and the actions will create a manifestation of that $1000 in your Prosperity Bank. The word of God says, *"Faith without WORKS (ACTION) is dead, being alone (or by itself) with no manifestation."James 2:20* If you have dropped the ball these 26 days then it's time to pick it back up and start back to running once again. Whichever day you stopped at it's time to start again. We have 64 days left let's MAKE IT HAPPEN!

In closing keep the faith and keep a mindset of expectation and anticipation, daily visualizing your goal as already reached and seeing yourself in possession of $1000. Talk with you tomorrow morning with another great challenge.

SAVE $1000 IN 90 DAYS CHALLENGE

Chapter 27

DAY 27 CHALLENGE & CONCLUSION

God bless you and good morning. Welcome to Day 27 of the **"Save $1000 in 90-Days Challenge."** Are you ready for your twenty seventh day of challenge to help you save $1000 in the next 90 Days?

TODAY'S WORD

FAITH. In order to achieve your goal of saving $1000 in 90 days it's going to take faith. What is faith? *"Now faith is the substance of things hoped for, the evidence of things not seen." Hebrews: 11:1* In other words faith is first off NOW not tomorrow or next week but now, you believe that what you desire you have it now. Second, faith is the assurance that you shall receive that which you're hoping for even though you don't see it before you at the present time. Third, faith moves you to action; you do something when you have faith because faith without works is DEAD! James 2:20 So continue to save that money in your Prosperity Bank and continue to WORK these challenges.

DAY 27 CHALLENGE

Put the largest bill you can afford in your prosperity bank today.

This is truly a challenge to take and put the largest bill that you can afford into your Prosperity Bank, but while you're doing it ask yourself what will this do for me? The bottom line is it will add to the bottom line and get you that much closer to achieving your goal of saving $1000 in 90 days. Have active faith not passive faith, do something and you're making something happen and breaking the back of insufficiency in your life.

CONCLUSION

Down 27 Days on the "Save $1000 in 90-Day Challenge." Are you operating in faith or are you operating in fear?

TONIGHT'S WORD

Faith says yes and goes forward, procrastinates, waits on perfect conditions and is afraid to go forth. Faith will enable you to save. Fear will wait and end up with nothing or next to nothing. Fear will stop you in your tracks. Faith will get you this...$1000 in 90 days! YES!!!!!

Chapter 28

DAY 28 CHALLENGE & CONCLUSION

God bless you and good morning. Welcome to Day 28 of the **"Save $1000 in 90-Days Challenge."** Are you ready for your twenty eighth day of challenge to help you save $1000 in the next 90 Days?

TODAY'S WORD

TITHES. The word tithe is seen throughout the Old Testament as well as the new in reference to man bringing God a tenth of his income. The scripture says, *"Bring ye all the tithes into the storehouse, that there may be meat in mine house, and prove me now herewith, saith the Lord of hosts, if I will not open you the windows of heaven, and pour you out a blessing, that there shall not be room enough to receive it."* Malachi 3:10

DAY 28 CHALLENGE

Bring the tithes to the house of God.

When you bring the tithes to the house of

God, He will in return bless the 90% that you have left and will enable you to do more with the 90% than you were able to do with the 100%.

But what mankind has failed to realize in all this is that when God opens up those windows, it's not money that will come raining down. What God will give you is wisdom, knowledge and understanding about how to make money and how to save money. Many are waiting for their ship to come in but the ship is not coming from afar because the ship is already in your possession. You have been given everything you need to prosper and see financial increase in your life. The wisdom that God gives you will come through his word, ideas, strategies, plans, concepts, principles etc..., about how to make money and save money so that you can have abundance. Jesus came that you *might have life and have it more abundantly. John 10:10*

But if you never learn to save, you will be in the poor house all the days of your life. These daily challenges tell you what to do and how to do it but they will not do it for you. Tithe and watch increase grow in your Prosperity Bank.

Chapter 29

DAY 29 CHALLENGE AND CONCLUSION

God bless you and good morning. Welcome to Day 29 of the **"Save $1000 in 90-Days Challenge."** Are you ready for your twenty ninth day of challenge to help you save $1000 in the next 90 Days?

TODAY'S WORD

STAY FOCUSED. Keep your eyes on the prize and don't be moved by what's going on around you. The prize is $1000 in 90 days and as long as you stay focused and continue to apply these challenges you will attain the prize. The bestselling book of all times (the Bible) tells us how to run in a race to obtain the prize, it says, *"Know ye not that they which run in a race run all, but one receiveth the prize? So run, that ye may obtain." 1 Corinthians 9:24*

In this race to obtain $1000 in 90 days, the way to run that you may obtain is to keep applying the daily challenges to your life that apply.

- Go the extra mile.
- Make the necessary sacrifices.
- Don't just be a spectator--Be a participator.
- Don't just read these daily challenges--Do them.
- Put that money aside instead of spending it on something non-essential.
- Your only competition is your old way of saving and spending.
- Stay focused on the new financial look that you will have in 90 days--A $1000 look and a new frame of mind about saving.

Don't just run with us in this 90 days challenge but run that you may obtain. See you at the finish line with $1000 in hand!

DAY 29 CHALLENGE

Start making money by turning your phone into a credit card machine.

We're living in the day of technology and it's time to start using it to your advantage. There is a way that you can begin to get paid anywhere and make money that will go into your account within 48-72 hours. There is money out there for you, be ready every way to receive it! Have you ever heard of Paypal Here or Square?

Begin to use your phone by getting a Paypal Here or Square Credit Card Reader that you can use on your phone to receive payment from people that may want to pay you what they owe you or purchase something from you using their credit cards. In the coming days we're going to show you how to never miss a sell or to be ready to receive monies at all times. I personally use the Paypal Here and Square and they have been wonderful and the money goes right into my account. Here is more information about how to get them and they're both   free. https://www.paypal.com/webapps/mpp/credit-card-reader
https://squareup.com/?gclid=CIGv__Lemb0C FS1eOgodSnwAWQ&sro=1

CONCLUSION

Save $1000 In 90 Days Challenge

Down 29 Days on the "Announcing the Save $1000 in 90-Day Challenge." When you stay focused on something you make sure to give your attention to that thing.

TONIGHT'S WORD

Continue to stay focused and in 61 days you will be rejoicing all the way to the bank. You will break yourself away from those terrible statistics and will no longer be in the 46% that has less than $800 in savings or part of the 22% that has less than $100 in savings. You're on your way and that is just the beginning.

Chapter 30

DAY 30 CHALLENGE & CONCLUSION

God bless you and good morning. Welcome to Day 30 of the **"Save $1000 in 90-Days Challenge."** Are you ready for your thirtieth day of challenge to help you save $1000 in the next 90 Days?

TODAY'S WORD

FREQUENCY. Can you believe that we are on day 30 already? If you have been following the challenges and applying them I know that you are amazed at your Prosperity Bank by now. But this is just the beginning. Some of you probably have hundreds of dollars in your Prosperity Bank now and you should but just in case you don't, don't stop we have sixty days to go.

We have reached a milestone of 30 consistent days of being steadfast with the challenges and folks I tell you its working. We're giving you information about how to *SAVE MONEY*--how to *MAKE MONEY – and how to SAVE THE MONEY YOU MAKE.* This is INFORMATION AT IT'S FINEST that others would charge HUNDREDS for you to know but I want you to know it because I want to see you come out of debt, living paycheck to paycheck, break the back of poverty, etc... But it all starts with you FIRST saving and having $1000 in your possession.

The word for today is FREQUENCY. The reason the majority of people in American, 46% have less than $800 and 22% have less than $100 is because people are tuned into the wrong frequency to break free. If you want to tune into a gospel station on the radio then you have to be on the correct frequency for gospel. A radio wave is an electromagnetic wave propagated by an antenna. Radio waves have different frequencies, and by tuning a radio receiver to a specific frequency you can pick up a specific signal.

Through these 90 day challenges we are helping you to tune your frequency in to another wave-the wave of *SAVING MONEY MAKING MONEY – AND SAVING THE*

MONEY THAT YOU MAKE. I can't make you save it or make it but if you will apply the challenges they will translate to money in your Prosperity Bank. STAY ON THIS FREQUENCY AND NEVER GET OFF--STAY TUNED!

DAY 30 CHALLENGE

Sell an item that somebody has been asking you about.

Some of us have items, things that individuals may have asked us to sell to them that we've been holding on to for years. It could be a car, a piece of furniture, a old cell phone, a collector's item, old DVD's, old books, etc... Is there something that somebody has been asking you to sell them for a while. If it's not something that you must keep in the family-- SELL IT-- and get the money and put it in your Prosperity Bank to help reach your goal of $1000. Life isn't forever, things come and go but you must know how to win in the game of life and many people are holding on to things that could help them get out of debt, into savings and on the road to Prosperity. Make it happen for you and your family.

CONCLUSION

Down 30 Days on the "Save $1000 in 90-Day Challenge." Keep your eye on the prize and what you are sowing you will surely reap.

TONIGHT'S WORD

I am very happy to see us reaching the milestone of 30 days of consistent challenges that will put money in your pocket. I want each of you to know that no matter where you were 30 days ago you are further now than you've ever been, but the best is yet to come. We're on a mission to help you break free from the statistics and it doesn't matter what your income is you can save $1000 in 90 days with these challenges.

But you can't just sit back and wait for something to happen you have to go forth and make something happen. The opportunities are here every day and we will be bringing you exciting challenges, some of them you will be able to make money right on your phone.

In closing keep the faith and keep a mindset

of expectation and anticipation, daily visualizing your goal as already reached and seeing yourself in possession of $1000. Talk with you tomorrow morning with another great challenge.

Chapter 31

DAY 31 CHALLENGE & CONCLUSION

God bless you and good morning. Welcome to Day 31 of the **"Save $1000 in 90-Days Challenge."** Are you ready for your thirty first day of challenge to help you save $1000 in the next 90 Days?

TODAY'S WORD

Someone stated *"If you want things in your life to change then you must change the things in your life."* This is what we've been emphasizing since day 1. You can't keep doing the same things but expect different results. If you want something that you've never had then you must do something that you've never done. A good example is what we challenge you to do on day 1--DON'T SPEND YOUR MONEY DURING YOUR BREAK TIMES-BUT SAVE IT! If this is something that you've been doing at least 3 days out of the week that alone has put a good amount of money in your Prosperity Bank.

Only those that are willing to accept change will see change. Saving $1000 in 90 days is not hard but it does require CHANGE. What you were doing before did not put $1000 in your saving within the last 180 days, 365 days, and for some within the last 1,095 days or the last 3 years. But continue to follow these challenges and do the ones that apply or that you can apply and you will see $1000 in your Prosperity Bank in 90 days.

DAY 31 CHALLENGE

Turn your hobby into cash.

A hobby is an activity or interest pursued for pleasure or relaxation and not as a main occupation. What hobby do you have that you love to do? What is that one thing that you do that others raves about and you're good at? Is it cooking, working on computers, making things, stamp collecting, wood carving, collecting things, making dollhouses, making music, dog training or breeding, building model ships or trains, scrapbooking, jewelry making, baking, doing hair, etc.. The list is almost endless and what you are doing as a hobby others are getting paid for their hobby, why not you? Whatever you're doing people will gladly pay you for it. Get busy now and start making money and begin to save the money that you make. Somebody have your $1000 and they're waiting for you to come and get it from them as you TURN YOUR HOBBY INTO CASH MONEY!

CONCLUSION

Down 31 Days on the "Save $1000 in 90-Day Challenge." Where you were 31 days ago is not important, because financially you're further today than you've ever been.

TONIGHT'S WORD

The word on today was such a life changing word if you allow it to be that I will simply reiterate it for your edification tonight. Someone stated "*If you want things in your life to change then you must change the things in your life.*"

In closing keep the faith and keep a mindset of expectation and anticipation, daily visualizing your goal as already reached and seeing yourself in possession of $1000. Talk with you tomorrow morning with another great challenge.

Chapter 32

DAY 32 CHALLENGE & CONCLUSION

God bless you and good morning. Welcome to Day 32 of the **"Save $1000 in 90-Days Challenge."** Are you ready for your thirty second day of challenge to help you save $1000 in the next 90 Days?

TODAY'S WORD

HABIT. The word habit is defined as: a settled or regular tendency or practice, esp. one that is hard to give up. Also it means to: Have an acquired behavior pattern regularly followed until it has become almost involuntary:

There are good habits and there are bad habits, if you have less than a $1000 in savings and living paycheck to paycheck you have a bad financial habit. In order to break this settled or regular tendency or practice that is causing you financial death daily you must replace it with a new habit.

Save $1000 In 90 Days Challenge

You must acquire a new behavior pattern regularly followed until IT becomes almost involuntary.

- Are you tired of living paycheck to paycheck?
- Are you tired of not having money in a savings?
- Are you tired of having to borrow money from others?

Then you must fight for your finances as never before. It's time out for being a wimp it's time to become a lion on a mission that will kill off any bad habits that is causing you financial death. It doesn't matter if you've tried to save numerous times. You may have gotten off course during this 90 day challenge but GET BACK UP AND KEEP FIGHTING FOR THE FINANCIAL LIFE YOU DESERVE.

You must get tired of being a part of the bad statistics because of bad financial habits.

- Researchers say 76 percent of Americans are living paycheck-to-paycheck.

- Twenty-seven percent have no savings.

These challenges are for you, it's time to put money in a savings and our mission is to show you how to save $1000 in 90 days.

DAY 32 CHALLENGE

Take the largest bill that you can afford and put it into your prosperity bank today.

Keep in mind that we're not in competition with any other person, only with our old bad habits. Our goal is to break away from those regular tendencies, practices and patterns that have kept us down financially. If you follow this challenge you are establishing a new habit of saving that will bless your bottom line-- which is more money in your Prosperity Bank.

NOTE: If you can't put a bill in today, make sure you put one in before the next 5 days and your Prosperity Bank will thank you at the end of 90 days. IF IT'S TO BE--IT'S UP TO YOU! (No one else is responsible for your savings but you).

CONCLUSION

Down 32 Days on the "Save $1000 in 90-Day Challenge." Where you are mentally is where you will be on Day 90.

TONIGHT'S WORD

Do you see yourself accomplishing your goal of saving $1000 in 90 days or are you wondering if you will accomplish your goal of saving $1000 in 90 days. We become what we think about. *"For As he (or she) thinketh in his (their) heart, so is he (they)." Proverbs 23:7* Think $1000 in your Prosperity Bank.

In closing keep the faith and keep a mindset of expectation and anticipation, daily visualizing your goal as already reached and seeing yourself in possession of $1000. Talk with you tomorrow morning with another great challenge.

Chapter 33

DAY 33 CHALLENGE & CONCLUSION

God bless you and good morning. Welcome to Day 33 of the **"Save $1000 in 90-Days Challenge."** Are you ready for your thirty third day of challenge to help you save $1000 in the next 90 Days?

TODAY'S WORD

The reason people fail financially in life is because they never learn how to give shape and structure to their finances. Follow the shape and structure and financial increase and prosperity is automatically yours. Avoid the shape and structure (or try to make up a new shape and structure) and your financial future will always end in chaos and confusion.

If your finances don't have shape and structure then they have difference and disorganization. And when these two things have the preeminence in your finances then you'll experience no savings, lack, poverty, barely making ends meet and pay-check to paycheck living. The reasons that people are experience these things throughout their life are because:

- The majority of individuals have either avoided the shape and structure.

- Tried to make up a new shape and structure.

- Or have not come into the knowledge of what the shape and structure is.

It's not how much money you make or don't make in life, it's how much you save, and the majority of people have not saved anything. Saving puts shape and structure into your financial experience and when you break the cycle of wasting and apply the principle of saving then your financial life automatically changes. This 90 day challenge is about showing you how to save, how to make money and how to save what you make.

DAY 33 CHALLENGE

Become a tutor.

Are you good at math, science, reading or any other subject that you can teach? You don't need a degree to become a tutor, you just need to know your subject thoroughly and have patience to teach it to kids that need your help. Parents are willing to pay you to tutor their kids, begin to advertise yourself at schools, online, etc... Tutors can make $10-15 an hour and this is money in your Prosperity Bank.

CONCLUSION

Down 33 Days on the "Save $1000 in 90-Day Challenge." The $1000 that you are expecting to save in 90 days is also expecting you to save it in 90 days. No room for failure!

TONIGHT'S WORD

The $1000 that you will save in this 90 day challenge will revolutionize your financial life. The $1000 is just the beginning. The success of saving this $1000 will open all kind of financial doors for you. When you achieve this goal you will be able to achieve any other financial goal--because after this the belief will be there.

Many people are hoping to become a millionaire one day but they can't even save a $1000. You have to achieve smaller goals first and these smaller goals will equip, fortify, empower your belief system to achieve bigger goals. The word of God says, *"For who hath despised the day of small things?" Zechariah 4:10* If you can achieve this small goal then bigger things await. We're just getting started you will have more money than you've had in the last 5, 10, 15 years or more if you will continue to apply these daily challenges and when the 90 days are up, there are more great things to come with bigger financial goals.

In closing keep the faith and keep a mindset of expectation and anticipation, daily visualizing your goal as already reached and seeing yourself in possession of $1000. Talk with you tomorrow morning with another great challenge.

CHAPTER 34

DAY 34 CHALLENGE & CONCLUSION

God bless you and good morning. Welcome to Day 34 of the **"Save $1000 in 90-Days Challenge."** Are you ready for your thirty fourth day of challenge to help you save $1000 in the next 90 Days?

TODAY'S WORD

The $1000 that you will save in this 90 day challenge will revolutionize your financial life. The $1000 is just the beginning. The success of saving this $1000 will open all kind of financial doors for you. When you achieve this goal you will be able to achieve any other financial goal-- because after this the belief will be there.

Without belief you don't have the confidence to achieve greater financial goals but with confidence in tact you're ready to excel. Each of these challenges accomplished will breathe more confidence, encouragement, empowerment, and attainment for greater things. You will believe you are invincible and that no financial goal can stand in your way. Our objective through these challenges is to get your mindset to a state of continuous belief that financial increase is just a state of mind. At the end of these 90 days you will be so empowered that you will be on a mission to help empower others to save their first $1000.

DAY 34 CHALLENGE

Take the largest bill that you can afford and put it into your prosperity bank today.

You already have money in your possession; you just have not been taking out any amount in putting it aside in a savings. The challenge for today is to take out that bill and put it aside--you may even have to sacrifice something that you were planning, but remember, whatever else you do with your money today, it won't be going into your Prosperity Bank but into someone else's Prosperity Bank. SAVE!

TONIGHT'S WORD

Every day that you put money into your Prosperity Bank you are getting that much closer to reaching your $1000 goal. You should be very excited about the way your bank is looking. Continue to follow the challenges and you will see progress, daily, weekly and monthly.

In closing keep the faith and keep a mindset of expectation and anticipation, daily visualizing your goal as already reached and seeing yourself in possession of $1000. Talk with you tomorrow morning with another great challenge.

CHAPTER 35

DAY 35 CHALLENGE & CONCLUSION

God bless you and good morning. Welcome to Day 35 of the **"Save $1000 in 90-Days Challenge."** Are you ready for your thirty fifth day of challenge to help you save $1000 in the next 90 Days?

TODAY'S WORD

CHANGE. The thing about change is that it just doesn't automatically happen for the better. Things can go from bad to worse but rarely does it goes from bad to good without you making some effort to bring forth good into your life. The sad things is that MOST people are sitting around waiting for a financial change to just happen for them but the only thing that will just happen is that your finances will go from bad to worse. So the word I have for today is a statement that I heard from someone else that is powerful and can change your finances and your life. I will repeat it several times with the hopes that it will get in your spirit, renew your mind and move you to action as never before. Here it is:

If you want things in your life to change then you must change the things in your life.

If you want things in your life to change then you must change the things in your life.

If you want things in your life to change then you must change the things in your life.

If you want things in your life to change then you must change the things in your life.

If you want things in your life to change then you must change the things in your life.

If you want things in your life to change then you must change the things in your life.

If you want things in your life to change then you must change the things in your life.

If you want things in your life to change then you must change the things in your life.

If you want things in your life to change then you must change the things in your life.

If you want things in your life to change then you must change the things in your life.

DAY 35 CHALLENGE

Automate savings.

Automate an emergency fund. Having an emergency fund is an essential part of your financial stability. Even when you are in debt, you still need to put money into an emergency fund because this can keep you from accumulating even more debt. A great way to get started is by automating your savings. You can have money transferred right out of your checking account into a savings account each pay period. An online savings account is a great place to stash your cash.

CONCLUSION

Down 35 Days on the "Save $1000 in 90-Day Challenge." The prosperity that you're creating will last you a life time.

TONIGHT'S WORD

The prosperity that you're creating today is more than just about money, you are being informed, enlighten and empowered. The knowledge that you're acquiring through these challenges will educate you about how to save money, make money and save the money you make. And once you've save $1000 you can do it again and again, because now you're informed and empowered.

In closing keep the faith and keep a mindset of expectation and anticipation, daily visualizing your goal as already reached and seeing yourself in possession of $1000. Talk with you tomorrow morning with another great challenge.

Chapter 36

DAY 36 CHALLENGE

God bless you and good morning. Welcome to Day 36 of the **"Save $1000 in 90-Days Challenge."** Are you ready for your thirty sixth day of challenge to help you save $1000 in the next 90 Days?

TODAY'S WORD

APPLICATION. Either you're applying these challenges and adding money to your Prosperity Bank or you're neglecting these challenges and you're bank is decreasing and shrinking. The word application means the action of putting something into operation.

When you take an active part then you can expect to blossom, flourish, gain, thrive, multiply, advance, increase, get on, gain and for things to turn out well. As we said before, if you do nothing you will not go from bad to good but from bad to worse. If you want things in your life to change then you must change the things in your life

DAY 36 CHALLENGE

Turn your coins into cash.

Do you have a lot of loose change but don't want to take the time to count it all? Then why not turn it into cash and deposit the cash into your Prosperity Bank. We've all seen the Coinstar machines in various stores. You take your coins in a jar or whatever you have them in and pour them in the machine and it gives you a receipt which you take to the checkout and get cash. They charge you a percentage from your coins and give you the rest. If you don't want to count all those coins then here's your answer. Don't forget that the cash you receive goes into your Prosperity Bank not your pocket to spend.

For additional information go here.
https://www.coinstar.com/#services

Chapter 37

DAY 37 CHALLENGE & CONCLUSION

God bless you and good morning. Welcome to Day 37 of the **"Save $1000 in 90-Days Challenge."** Are you ready for your thirty seventh day of challenge to help you save $1000 in the next 90 Days?

TODAY'S WORD

THOUGHTS. This word is defined as the action or process of thinking. Everything in your life you've created with your thoughts (thinking) first. If you are a part of the statistics where "46% have less than $800 and 22% have less than $100 in savings" you're there because of your thinking and your actions.

The word of God *states "For as he thinketh in his heart, so is he." Proverbs 23:7a* In other words you are where you are financially because your thinking has made it so. You can't think one way and then expect another way to manifest. If your finances have been bad it's because your thinking and actions have been bad. If you have nothing or less than $50 in your Prosperity Bank in the 37th day of this challenge it's because your thinking and your actions have been contrary to the challenge and you are still thinking and acting just like you did before the challenge.

Remember, "*If you want the things in your life to change then you must change the things in your life.*" This challenge will put $1000 in your savings in 90 days but you have to think thoughts that believe and know that it will. We become what we think about. Think--"I shall have $1000 in my savings in 90 days" and have the corresponding actions and let that thought become an obsession, a burning desire to see that $1000 manifest in your Prosperity Bank and you will LAUGH all the way to the BANK.

DAY 37 CHALLENGE

Shop around for better deals on your life, auto, home and health insurance.

You may be spending a lot more money than you need to on insurances. Check around to see if you can get a better deal that will save you hundreds of dollars a year. When you find better deals then put the difference of the money that you were spending in your savings to help you reach your $1000 savings goal.

Chapter 38

DAY 38 CHALLENGE

God bless you and good morning. Welcome to Day 38 of the **"Save $1000 in 90-Days Challenge."** Are you ready for your thirty eighth day of challenge to help you save $1000 in the next 90 Days?

TODAY'S WORD

WANT. A key element in obtaining money is that you must first want money. Many may observe this statement and say--"well everyone wants more money." Well the word want is defined as: having a desire to possess or do (something), in this case having or possessing $1000.

Many started out the challenge wanting to have $1000 in 90 days but only those that have turned their desire into a burning desire will actually possess or have it. Those that have this burning desire to have $1000 in 90 days are the ones that in their saving are:

1. On fire with their saving.

2. Very strong in their savings.
3. Very hot in their savings plan.
4. Intense in their savings.
5. Blazing   about   their   savings.

These are the ones that will have $1000 in their savings at the end of the 90 day challenge. Because desire alone has gotten you in the predicament that you were end before the challenge, but a on fire, strong, hot, intense, blazing and burning desire is what will get you out and put $1000 in your Prosperity Bank. The burning desire is not that I just want a thing, but I got to have it, I must have it, I shall have it. AND HAVE IT YOU SHALL!

DAY 38 CHALLENGE

Challenge for today buy in bulk.

When you buy things in bulk you are saving a great deal of money and purchasing goods in large amounts, typically at a discount price. Put the money you save into your Prosperity Bank.

Chapter 39

DAY 39 CHALLENGE & CONCLUSION

God bless you and good morning. Welcome to Day 39 of the **"Save $1000 in 90-Days Challenge."** Are you ready for your thirty ninth day of challenge to help you save $1000 in the next 90 Days?

TODAY'S WORD

LIE. A lie is defined as a false statement made with deliberate intent to deceive; an intentional untruth; a falsehood; an inaccurate or false statement. If you are part of the statistics where--46% of people have less than $800 in savings and 22% have less than $100 in savings, then you have fallen for the lie. The lie that have deceived you to believe that you can't save any money because of this or that.

However, in these 39 days of challenges we have set that lie to rest and our Prosperity Bank proves that truth prevails over lies when you take massive action to turn your situation around. No matter what your situation is, through these daily challenges you can save MONEY if you refuse to believe the lie and change your mind set. You can't keep believing the lie and expect truth to come forth. But if you know the truth and accept the truth and act on the truth--the Bible says, "you shall know the truth and the truth shall make you FREE." John 8:32

Look in your Prosperity Bank and if you have $100, $200, $300 or more--THAT'S FREEDOM BABY! And we still have 51 days to go. Remember, If you want things in your life to change then you must change the things in your life.

Day 39 CHALLENGE

Give up expensive habits.

Do you have expensive habits that are costing you a fortune over time? Habits such as CIGARETTES, ALCOHOL or DRUGS, these habits are one reason why you're not able to save money. The average smoker forks over at least $1,500 a year, and in other states, it's closer to $3000. Each year Americans spend more than $90 billion on alcohol. In marijuana spending it is estimated that $10 billion to over $120 billion a year is spent on marijuana.

And we still say we don't have money to save. Get some assistance and give up your expensive habits and STOP BELIEVING THE LIE!

Chapter 40

DAY 40 CHALLENGE

God bless you and good morning. Welcome to Day 40 of **the "Save $1000 in 90-Days Challenge."** Are you ready for your fortieth day of challenge to help you save $1000 in the next 90 Days?

TODAY'S WORD

WILLING. Most individuals want a financial change but many are not willing to do what it takes to see the change manifest. The word willing is defined as: ready, eager, or prepared to do something. Most people confuse desire with willing--they desire a financial change (even though it's a weak desire) but they're not willing, ready, eager or prepared TO DO SOMETHING to make it happen.

The Bible even tells us about willing being the only way to see change, saying, *"If ye be willing and obedient, ye shall eat the good of the land: (ye shall prosper, have, increase and the land will yield to you it's goodness) But if ye refuse and rebel (if you're not willing), ye shall be devoured (wiped out, destroyed, overwhelmed, devastated) with the sword: (you will suffer, lack, poverty, pay check living, NO SAVINGS) for the mouth of the Lord hath spoken it." Isaiah 1: 19-20*

A desire is not enough to go from no savings or a little to $1000 in 90 days. You must be willing, ready, and eager and prepared to do something to make it happen.

DAY 40 CHALLENGE

Cancel any channels on your satellite or cable that you don't watch or cancel your cable / satellite all together.

You may have many channels that you don't watch or only watch here and there, cancel them and begin to save that money in your Prosperity Bank. You can even cancel your service all together and get Clear TV by going to the website listed at: (http://www.cleartv.com/?gclid=CLn_oZL6tb 0CFYuXOgodMGMAiA) and save yourself a bundle.

CONCLUSION

Down 40 Days on the "Announcing the Save $1000 in 90-Day Challenge." This $1000 challenge is challenging you every day to get out of your comfort zone.

TONIGHT'S WORD

Are you willing to do things differently or are you going to keep doing the same old same old? The same old same old has gotten you where you are today, something different will bring different results.

In closing keep the faith and keep a mindset of expectation and anticipation, daily visualizing your goal as already reached and seeing yourself in possession of $1000. Talk with you tomorrow morning with another great challenge.

SAVE $1000 IN 90 DAYS CHALLENGE

Chapter 41

DAY 41 CHALLENGE

God bless you and good morning. Welcome to Day 41 of the **"Save $1000 in 90-Days Challenge."** Are you ready for your forty first day of challenge to help you save $1000 in the next 90 Days?

TODAY'S WORD

Before you can get where you want to be you must deal with where you are!

Many times people want big things like a million dollars but they have not learned the simple truth of how to save even $1000. If truth be told with no presumption allowed, you don't have faith or belief for a million dollars. Because if you had TRUE FAITH AND BELIEF you would have it. *"And Jesus said unto them, Because of your unbelief: for verily I say unto you, If ye have faith as a grain of mustard seed, ye shall say unto this mountain, Remove hence to yonder place; and it shall remove; and nothing shall be impossible unto you." Matthew 17:20*

If the truth be told you don't even feel like you can have a million dollars in your possession right now. You have to stop deceiving ourselves because your deception has not manifested what you think you believe and have faith for. You call it faith but it's not faith, it's foolishness and presumption. Listen, faith manifest, faith does not fail. Faith produces action and faith without works is dead.

The word for today is don't try to believe for a million dollars, you don't even feel like you can have a million dollars right now. If you tell yourself right now "I will have a million dollars the thought that will come back to you is unbelief and doubt. And how you feel is 99% of the importance to manifesting what you believe for. But if you have been following the words for today through these challenges and actively doing the challenges that fit you---if you tell yourself right now "I will have $1000 in 90 days you believe it and thoughts of faith and belief come back to you. You will have not what you think you deserve or want but what you have true faith for, true belief for and have a true feel for.

Some may want to dispute and say--"No I do have faith for a million." I say to you go back 41 days and look in your bank account and see what you had prior to your start. Now look in your Prosperity bank at what you've been doing for 41 days and see what you have. During this challenge you've dealt with reality and from your start you've actively participated and manifested what you now have--Praise God. You are on your way!

DAY 41 CHALLENGE

Take the largest bill that you can afford and put it into your prosperity bank.

This is adding to the bottom line and you're increasing your income more and more. If you can't add anything today just may a vow to yourself that when you get monies again you will add that bill to your Prosperity Bank right away, whether it's $1, $5, $10, $20 or $100.

Chapter 42

Day 42 CHALLENGE & CONCLUSION

God bless you and good afternoon. Welcome to Day 42 of the **"Save $1000 in 90-Days Challenge."** Are you ready for your forty second day of challenge to help you save $1000 in the next 90 Days?

TODAY'S WORD

CREATE THE FUTURE YOU WANT. The way to create the future you want is to write out the future you want on paper. When you write it out then you're renewing your mind and causing a transformation in your psyche. The Bible says, " *Write the vision, and make it plain upon tables, that he may run that readeth it.*" *Habakkuk 2:2* When you write it out you are creating the future because your renewed mind will cause you now to anticipate increase. The more you write it out the more it becomes real to you and it will manifest in your life.

DAY 42 CHALLENGE

Save $1000 In 90 Days Challenge

Write out your financial desire on paper.

Your challenge for today is to write out your financial goal as already accomplished. Write it out in this manner "I have saved $1000 in my Prosperity Bank." Write it out at least 25 times in a notebook on a daily basis, not your iPad, iPhone or any electronic gadget, use good old pen (pencil) and paper. WRITE IT OUT WITH PEN (PENCIL) AND PAPER AND WATCH WHAT BEGINS TO HAPPEN.

Down 42 Days on the "Announcing the Save $1000 in 90 Days Challenge." At this very moment you are either been attracted or repelled to your $1000.

TONIGHT'S WORD

You can be assured that you are being repelled when you think and say such things:

- It's hard to save money.
- It seems like I'm destined to struggle.
- I barely make enough to pay my bills.
- How am I going to save when I'm living paycheck to paycheck.

- Times are tough.

You can be assured that you are attracting your $1000 when you think and say such things as:

- I can save that $1000.
- Things are turning around in my favor.
- Each day I'm getting closer to my $1000 savings.
- I am well able to save and fulfill my challenge.
- It's a great time to save.

You attract what you think about and talk about most of the time. Talk $1000 in your Prosperity Bank and $1000 you shall have.

In closing keep the faith and keep a mindset of expectation and anticipation, daily visualizing your goal as already reached and seeing yourself in possession of $1000. Talk with you tomorrow morning with another great challenge.

Chapter 43

DAY 43 CHALLENGE & CONCLUSION

God bless you and good morning. Welcome to Day 43 of the "Save $1000 in 90-Days Challenge." Are you ready for your forty third day of challenge to help you save $1000 in the next 90 Days?

TODAY'S WORD

MONEY. Money is the number one medium of exchange and therefore the majority of our lives are wrapped up in the aspect of money one way or another. Therefore, we use money on a consistent basis and the majority of time when you leave your house you will spend money in some aspect. You cannot get away from the use of money in your daily life so therefore it seems logical that our desire should be to have more money in our lives than less money.

Money begets money, when you have money in your possession more money will come to you. When you don't have money then money is repelled from you, for some reason money doesn't like to stay in the possession of those that don't have it. In the Bible it says, "*The rich man's wealth is his strong city: the destruction of the poor is their poverty.*" *Proverbs 10:15*

What is hurting the poor is being poor, therefore the poor have to get money in their possession. The first monies that a poor person need is to save $1000, when you can save $1000 a whole new avenue of monies begin to open up for you. This is the reason that we have the Save $1000 in 90 Days Challenge, we're using this challenge to help all that really want to break the financial barrier to do it with this challenge. If you can get here and save $1000 you can get anywhere financially with the right wisdom, knowledge and understanding. Proverbs 23:3-4

DAY 43 CHALLENGE

Having money in your possession.

Having $1000 in your Prosperity Bank is of utmost importance, you can witness to the fact that when you have even a little extra money it makes you feel good knowing that you have a little extra left over. How do you think you would feel if you had an extra $1000 in your Savings? Wouldn't it make you feel more stable and powerful in life. Poor people that have no savings and living paycheck to paycheck don't feel powerful and in control of life, they feel out of control and powerless. To these individuals life is whipping them and they're feeling financially destitute and less than adequate in their finances. You have to have money in your possession and you start by saving $1000. Follow and do the CHALLENGES because they are designed to PUT MONEY IN YOUR POSSESSION! Can you say "$1000 in my Possession?"

Down 43 Days on the "Announcing the Save $1000 in 90 Days Challenge." You are one day closer to your $1000 in manifestation.

Tonight's Word

A continual word is: If you want the things in your life to change then you have to change the things in your life. Are you putting into action the challenges or are you just reading them daily. Reading them alone will not add to the bottom line because faith without works is dead, being alone.

In closing keep the faith and keep a mindset of expectation and anticipation, daily visualizing your goal as already reached and seeing yourself in possession of $1000. Talk with you tomorrow morning with another great challenge.

Chapter 44

Day 44 CHALLENGE & CONCLUSION

God bless you and good morning. Welcome to Day 44 of **the "Save $1000 in 90-Days Challenge."** Are you ready for your forty fourth day of challenge to help you save $1000 in the next 90 Days?

TODAY'S WORD

TOMORROW. Someone said, "Remember, today is the tomorrow you worried about yesterday." Your worrying did not change anything about today, it just gave you something to do but it didn't get you anywhere. The only thing that will get you closer to your financial goal of saving $1000 in 90 days is by you taking massive ACTION to bring it to pass. If you want money in your Prosperity Bank you must:

1. Save
2. Apply the Challenges
3. Save
4. Apply the Challenges

5. Save
6. Apply the Challenges
7. Save

Just wishing, praying and hoping will not do it. You must put works behind your faith and when you do God intervenes to help you bring it to pass. God helps those that help themselves. When God created Adam it said, *"And the Lord God took the man, and put him into the garden of Eden to dress it and to keep it." Genesis 2:15* In other words ADAM take--ACTION--WORK--DO SOMETHING! Likewise if you want a $1000 in 90 days you must take--ACTION--WORK--DO SOMETHING and it will come to pass.

DAY 44 CHALLENGE

Buy a roll of quarters between today and Saturday and put them in your prosperity jar.

Anytime you're putting money in your Prosperity Jar you're adding to the bottom line and this is bringing you that much closer to your $1000 goal.

Buying a roll of quarters is taking massive action to get you where you want to be--AND THAT IS $1000 SAVED IN 90 DAYS!

Chapter 45

Day 45 CHALLENGE & CONCLUSION

God bless you and welcome to day 45 of the **"Save $1000 in 90 Days Challenge."** Are you ready for your forty fifth day of challenge to help you save $1000 in the next 90 days?

TODAY'S WORD

DEBT-FREE. If you want to live a life of debt free living then you must first learn to get your finances under control. The first step is saving for that $1000 for emergency. If you don't have a $1000 then when emergencies come up you will have to either borrow or use a credit card for the emergency. Once you accomplish this then your next step is learn how to eliminate your debts one at a time.

DAY 45 CHALLENGE

Take out the largest bill that you can afford to put aside and put it in your Prosperity Bank.

Save $1000 In 90 Days Challenge

Down 45 Days on the "Save $1000 in 90 Days Challenge." We're half way there and the best is yet to come.

Tonight's Word

I hope you had a chance to listen to the video today and you really took it to heart. You can change your financial situation but the change starts with you. No one is going to do it for you; you must do it for yourself.

In closing keep the faith and keep a mindset of expectation and anticipation, daily visualizing your goal as already reached and seeing yourself in possession of $1000.

Chapter 46

Day 46 CHALLENGE & CONSLUSION

God bless you and welcome to day 46 of the **"Save $1000 in 90 Days Challenge."** Are you ready for your forty sixth day of challenge to help you save $1000 in the next 90 days?

TODAY'S WORD

KEEP YOUR MIND OFF THE THINGS YOU DON'T WANT! The key to seeing things manifest in your life is that you must keep your mind off the things you don't want and on the things you do want. If you constantly keep your mind daily on what you don't want more of what you don't want will manifest in your life.

- If you don't want more lack then keep your mind off of lack.
- If you don't want poverty then keep your mind off of poverty.
- If you don't want financial struggles then keep your mind off of financial struggles.

What you keep your mind on mostly is what you will attract in your life.

- If you want more abundance then keep your mind on abundance.
- If you want more prosperity then keep your mind on prosperity.
- If you want more financial increase then keep your mind on financial increase.

"For as he thinketh in his heart, so is he." Proverb 23:7

DAY 46 CHALLENGE

Check your progress for the past 45 days.

Check your progress for the past 45 days and see if you have really done the challenges that fit you. See if you could have applied more effort to doing more of the challenges in order to put more money in your Prosperity Bank. Some things to look at in the remaining 44 days are:

- How much have you saved?

- What can you do to double your efforts on the remaining 44 days to make sure that you reach your $1000 goal?
- What challenges can you go back and do that you didn't do?

These closing 44 days—*Go after your goals with the determination like it's a matter of life and financial death.*

Down 46 Days on the "Announcing the Save $1000 in 90 Days Challenge." If it's to be it's up to me. (True saying for you.)

TONIGHT'S WORD

Make it happen, don't wait for it to happen. Those that just sit around and hope and wait will end up with nothing or next to nothing. *"He becometh poor that dealeth with a slack hand: but the hand of the diligent maketh rich." Proverbs 10:4*

In closing keep the faith and keep a mindset of expectation and anticipation, daily visualizing your goal as already reached and seeing yourself in possession of $1000. Talk with you tomorrow morning with another great challenge.

Chapter 47

Day 47 CHALLENGE & CONCLUSION

God bless you and good morning. Welcome to day 47 of the **"Save $1000 in 90 Days Challenge."** Are you ready for your forty seventh day of challenge to help you save $1000 in the next 90 days?

TODAY'S WORD

SOMEDAY. Many times when people think about changing their financial situation they will continue to put it off for sometime in the future. And that future date always ends up being NEVER. You have to get away from the SOMEDAY and make your financial change TODAY! If you do nothing your finances will not just change because you hope it will, you must take massive action to make it happen.

These challenges are designed to provoke you to action NOW, not tomorrow or sometime in the future but TODAY! Someday will always end up being NO DAY! Remember, if you want the things in your life to change then you must change the things in your life.

DAY 47 CHALLENGE

Lower your cell phone bill.

You may have things on your cell phone that you may be paying for but never use. You can lower your cell phone in many ways.

1. Shop around for a better deal

2. Try Straight talk—a set monthly bill with no overage. http:www.straighttalk.com

3. **Wal-mart Family Mobile**—you can have several phones, first phone line is $39.88 and each additional line you save $5. http://www.walmart.com once you are on the site then look for **"Electronics & Office."** Then go **to "Cell Phones & Services."**

4. Let your current carrier know that you're thinking about switching unless they can lower your bill.

5. Bundle.

With the extra money you save—you know what to do with it—SAVE IT—Put it in your Prosperity Bank.

Down 47 Days on the "Save $1000 in 90 Days Challenge."

TONIGHT'S WORD

Money Challenges. Using your receipts to make money was one of the challenges. Have you done this? If you haven't why not? If you're not using your receipts then you're not getting paid for something you already have in your possession. You're doing this right on your cell phone, how much easier can making money get?

In closing keep the faith and keep a mindset of expectation and anticipation, daily visualizing your goal as already reached and seeing yourself in possession of $1000. Talk with you tomorrow morning with another great challenge.

Chapter 48

Day 48 CHALLENGES & CONCLUSION

God bless you and good morning. Welcome to Day 48 of the **"Save $1000 in 90 Days Challenge."** Are you ready for your forty eighth day of challenge to help you save $1000 in the next 90 days?

TODAY'S WORD

IS MONEY GOOD OR BAD? According to the Bible "money answers all things" (meaning all natural things). If you have a natural situation, if you have the money that situation can be solved.

- Money will pay off those bills that are due.
- Money will help with the needs of life.
- Money will be a hedge about you and your family.
- Money will help you to feed the hungry.
- Money will enable you to not just settle in life.

Money is actually a blessing from God and the more of it you have the more of a blessing you can be to your family, others and your own life.

The Bible says, *"Every man also to whom God hath given riches and wealth, and hath given him power to eat thereof, and to take his portion, and to rejoice in his labour; this is the gift of God." Ecclesiastes 5:19*

DAY 48 CHALLENGE

Shop online for any big purchases.

Many times if you have to buy something you can get it cheaper if you purchase the same item online. Therefore make sure to search online before you make that purchase. And with the difference that you will save--put it in your Prosperity Bank--SAVINGS, SAVINGS, SAVINGS

Down 48 Days on the "Save $1000 in 90 Days Challenge."

TONIGHT'S WORD

If you want something that you never had then you must do something that you've never done.

Chapter 49

Day 49 CHALLENGE

God bless you and good evening. Welcome to Day 49 of the **"Save $1000 in 90-Days Challenge."** Are you ready for your forty ninth day of challenge to help you save $1000 in the next 90 Days?

TODAY'S WORD

SEED. When Sunday comes around you have an opportunity to go to the house of God. Make this your day to go and worship the Lord and when you go bring a seed in the form of money to give toward the work of God. When you give a seed then you can expect a harvest to come forth.

The Bible says, *"But this I say, He which soweth sparingly shall reap also sparingly; and he which soweth bountifully shall reap also bountifully."* 2 *Corinthians 9:6* When you sow today you will determine the harvest that you will reap in accordance to the seed you're sowing. And when you sow with expectation and anticipation that God is faithful that promised.

DAY 49 CHALLENGE

Sow a seed in the house of God.

The word of God gives us the answers to all of life issues, even finances. Don't think that God's not concerned with your finances; he is more concerned with them than you are and he says. *"Beloved, I wish above all things that thou mayest prosper and be in health, even as thy soul prospereth." 3 John 2*

Chapter 50

Day 50 CHALLENGE & CONCLUSION

God bless you and good evening. Welcome to Day 50 of the **"Save $1000 in 90-Days Challenge."** Are you ready for your fiftieth day of challenge to help you save $1000 in the next 90 Days?

TODAY'S WORD

POSSIBLE. The word possible means something that is able to be done. Something that's possible is something that can happen, something that has the potential to become what you want, or something capable of existing. It is possible for each of you to save $1000 in 90 days if you have been following the challenges. It does not matter what your circumstance are, it can happen if you will believe it and work towards making it happen. The person that believes it's possible and the person that believes it's impossible is both right. Which person are you?

DAY 50 CHALLENGE

Save $1000 In 90 Days Challenge

Spend less on entertainment this week.

We have 40 days left in the 90 day challenge and depending on where you are in your savings amount you need to really turn up the saving and making aspect of the challenge. So this week spend less on entertainment, here are some ideas:

- Go to a FREE CONCERT.
- Go to a FREE FESTIVAL.
- Go to a matinee instead of a later movie.
- Instead of going out for a later evening dinner-catch a dinner special.
- If all else fails--grab a pizza and a red box movie.

And of course you know what to do with the money that you save--PUT IT IN YOUR PROSPERITY BANK!

Down 50 Days on the "Announcing the Save $1000 in 90 Days Challenge."

TONIGHT'S WORD

Forty days to go and we're closer to accomplishing the $1000 challenge than ever before. At the end of these 90 days your financial life and your mindset will never be the same. Change is the key, these next 40 days become obsessed with saving and you will be smiling all the way to the bank.

In closing keep the faith and keep a mindset of expectation and anticipation, daily visualizing your goal as already reached and seeing yourself in possession of $1000. Talk with you tomorrow morning with another great challenge. Don't forget to check out the blog to catch up on any challenges that you may have missed.

Chapter 51

Day 51 CHALLENGE

God bless you and good evening. Welcome to Day 51 of the **"Save $1000 in 90-Days Challenge."** Are you ready for your fifty first day of challenge to help you save $1000 in the next 90 Days?

TODAY'S WORD

PRAYER. Another way to attract money into your life is by using the power of prayer. Many have been taught that we shouldn't pray for finances but according to the scriptures we can ask God for whatever we need (even money). The word of God says, *"Therefore I say unto you, What things (money fall in the things category) soever ye desire, when ye pray, believe that ye receive them, and ye shall have them."* Mark 11:24

When you pray for money pray with as much passion as you would if you were praying for your healing or anything else. The word of God says, *"ye have not, because ye ask not."* James 4:2c And when you pray for money don't pray out of lust or evil desires for money, to have money to waste and do wicked, crooked and evil things with. The word of God says, *"You ask, and receive not, because you ask amiss, that ye may consume it upon your lusts. James 4:3* Your asking in this case is so that you can have a savings of $1000 for emergency money and to start better managing your money. Don't just pray and ask for it once but ask and keep on asking until you receive the money that you're praying for. Jesus said, *"Ask, and it shall be given you; For everyone that asketh receiveth (that mean to ask and keep on asking until you receive.) Luke 11:5-10*

DAY 51 CHALLENGE

Pray over your money for the remaining 39 days and expect financial miracles.

Here is how to speak over your money and accounts to cause increase.

1. Take your money in your hands and say *"Wealth and riches are in my house now in Jesus name."*

2. Take your bankbook and speak over it saying, *"The blessing of the Lord are upon you now in Jesus name."*

3. Take your money in your hands and say, *"God is multiplying you now and increase and prosperity is upon you."*

4. Take your bankbook in your hands and say, *"The blessing of the Lord it maketh rich and I am blessed and rich today."*

5. Take your money in your hands and say, *"God is multiplying you now just as Jesus multiplied the fish and loaves."*

6. Take your bankbook in your hands and say, *"And we know that all things work together for good to them that love God, to them who are the called according to his purpose. Thank you Father that all things are working together in my bank account now.*

7. Take your money and bankbook in your hands and say, *"Money loves to fill my pocket and accounts and they are both filled now."*

Begin to do this on a daily basis over your money and accounts and watch God produce creative and miraculous miracles in your behalf.

Chapter 52

Day 52 CHALLENGE & CONCLUSION

God bless you and good morning. Welcome to Day 52 of the **"Save $1000 in 90-Days Challenge."** Are you ready for your fifty second day of challenge to help you save $1000 in the next 90 Days?

TODAY'S WORD

SPEAK ONLY BLESSING OVER YOUR LIFE TODAY! The word of God says, "Death and life are in the power of the tongue: and they that love it shall eat the fruit thereof." Proverbs 18:21 The one thing that defeats more people than anything else and is more powerful than any force on earth is the power of your words. Mankind everywhere is being defeated financially on a continuous basis by the words of their mouth. The words which you speak daily will either put you over in life financially or hold you in bondage financially. The words you speak with consistency will become a creative force in your finances and release the power of God within you to work on your behalf.

DAY 52 CHALLENGE

Speak only positive words over your finances for the next 38 days.

Start today and break loose by beginning to affirm that which will produce financially for you. Get rid of the negative words; get them out of your spirit, mind and vocabulary. Begin this day to speak spiritual faith filled words that's full of life, speak them with power and authority and watch your financial situation change before your eyes. Speak today.

- Today is a new day, another chance to begin again.
- Today I make the best of it and through Christ I win.
- Today is a new day, all things work together for my good, I am an heir of God and joint heir with Jesus Christ and all things work as they should.
- Today is a new day, with God's help I succeed, the key to my success

is persistence and with that all my financial goals are achieved.

- Today is a new day, one I have never before seen, it presents to me a new opportunity therefore I am observant and keen.
- Today is a new day, I face this day with Courage and belief, I now look beyond all negatives, today I have victory.
- Today is a new day, I live this day and fulfill my true intent, accomplishing my life plans, I'm now all that God meant.
- Today is a new day to confess my affirmations; I do this consistently and see the financial manifestation.

Down 52 Days on the "Save $1000 in 90 Days Challenge."

TONIGHT'S WORD

Don't forget to start SPEAKING ONLY POSITIVE WORDS OVER YOUR FINANCES FOR THE NEXT 38 DAYS.

Chapter 53

Day 53 CHALLENGE

God bless you and good evening. Welcome to Day 53 of the **"Save $1000 in 90-Days Challenge."** Are you ready for your fifty third day of challenge to help you save $1000 in the next 90 Days?

TODAY'S WORD

ABUNDANCE. The word abundance is defined as an extremely plentiful or over-sufficient quantity or supply. Life was never meant to be a struggle. The God of all creation is interested in you having a full supply and he sent his son Jesus Christ who stated *"I am come that they might have life, and that they might have it more abundantly."* John 10:10

Now you have to decide, do you want to continue to struggle in life or do you want the abundant life. If you want the abundant life then there are sacrifices that will have to be made and actions that will have to be taken. If you keep doing what everyone else is doing you're going to keep getting what everyone else is getting. Most individuals don't have $1000 in savings. You have to break away from the pack if you want change. Remember, if you want the things in your life to change then you must change the things in your life.

DAY 53 CHALLENGE

Ask for military or senior citizens discounts.

When you go out shopping for the remaining 37 days if you are military or a senior citizen make sure to ask for your discounts. There are hundreds of discounts for senior citizens and military that you probably don't even know about. Some stores even advertise that they have these discounts but most don't even think about it.

What will you do with this discount savings? Put it in your Prosperity Bank of course to add to your bottom line of saving $1000 in 90 days.

Chapter 54

Day 54 CHALLENGE & CONCLUSION

God bless you and good evening. Welcome to Day 54 of the **"Save $1000 in 90-Days Challenge."** Are you ready for your fifty third day of challenge to help you save $1000 in the next 90 Days?

TODAY'S WORD

EXPECTATION. Expectation is the missing key on the road to financial success. You will not get what you think you rightly deserve but you will receive what you believe and what you expect.

If you expect nothing then you will receive nothing. If you expect something then you will receive that which you're expecting. Expectation is like a magnet that will attract and draw to you that which you're anticipating, whether good or bad, so only expect good financially.

DAY 54 CHALLENGE

The $5 savings plan.

With this challenge the objective is every time you come across a $5 bill in your possession take and put it in your Prosperity bank. This challenge will enable you to quickly save $50-$100 within the next 30 days, adding to your bottom line.

Down 54 Days on the "Save $1000 in 90 Days Challenge."

TONIGHT'S WORD

36 DAYS TO CONCLUSION. At the end of the 90 days you will have both a changed bank account and a changed attitude about savings. The reason both of these things would have changed for you is because you realized that, If you want the things in your life to change; you must change the things in your life.

In closing keep the faith and keep a mindset of expectation and anticipation, daily visualizing your goal as already reached and seeing yourself in possession of $1000. Talk with you tomorrow morning with another great challenge.

Chapter 55

Day 55 CHALLENGE

God bless you and good evening. Welcome to Day 55 of the **"Save $1000 in 90-Days Challenge."** Are you ready for your fifty fifth day of challenge to help you save $1000 in the next 90 Days?

TODAY'S WORD

YOU GOT CASH. On my Paypal account when someone purchases something from me the email will come to my phone and say, YOU GOT CASH. Well, this is also a good motivational phrase to tell yourself on a daily basis--Dexter_____ (place your name there) YOU GOT CASH! What this will do is help to change your mindset that may be constantly telling you; _____ (place your name there) YOU NEED CASH (for this or that). If you are struggling financially your mindset has a struggling mentality and you have to renew your mind and break free from that mentality. What better way than to tell yourself--Dexter _____ (place your name there) YOU GOT

CASH!

DAY 55 CHALLENGE

Sell your used books.

Here is a sure way to get cash quick. You may have money just laying around the house that you can use to reach your goal of saving $1000 in 90 days. Do you have books such as?

- Textbooks
- Accounting Books
- Economic Books
- Science Books
- College Books of various kinds.
- Nursing Books
- Business Books
- Etc...

If you have any of these books there is a company that will pay you for those books and they pay well. Check out this website at: http://www.cash4books.net/ and get the money you need to add to your Prosperity Bank.

Chapter 56

Day 56 CHALLENGE

God bless you and good evening. Welcome to Day 56 of the **"Save $1000 in 90-Days Challenge."** Are you ready for your fifty sixth day of challenge to help you save $1000 in the next 90 Days?

TODAY'S WORD

SOURCE. The word source is defined as: someone or something that provides what is wanted or needed. The cause of something. Either you are your source or you allow God to be your source. If you allow God to be your source then you can look forward to God leading and guiding you to the things that you need in life. If you are your source then you will have to figure out all things yourself. Source is powerful but the ability of that power will depend on your source.

DAY 56 CHALLENGE

Make money blogging and then save the money you

make.

A blog is a discussion or informational site published on the World Wide Web and consisting of discrete entries ("posts") typically displayed in reverse chronological order (the most recent post appears first). If you are well informed on a particular subject you can turn it into a subject that may be worthy of blogging.

A majority are interactive, allowing visitors to leave comments and even message each other via GUI widgets on the blogs, and it is this interactivity that distinguishes them from other static websites.[2] In that sense, blogging can be seen as a form of social networking service. Indeed, bloggers do not only produce content to post on their blogs, but also build social relations with their readers and other bloggers.[3] There are high-readership blogs which do not allow comments, such as Daring Fireball.

Chapter 57

Day 57 CHALLENGE

God bless you and good evening. Welcome to Day 57 of the **"Save $1000 in 90-Days Challenge."** Are you ready for your fifty seventh day of challenge to help you save $1000 in the next 90 Days?

TODAY'S WORD

The money you save today is the agreement you made with yourself at the beginning of the 90 day challenge. Reevaluate your priorities and get back on track for these remaining 33 days. Some people have saved $1000 in 30 days, you can do it just get back focused.

DAY 57 CHALLENGE

Ditch your land line / home phone.

In this day and time just about everyone of age of have a cell phone. A home phone in many cases is unnecessary and just another added expense. This is money that you could be putting in your Prosperity Bank monthly. You could save an extra $30-$45 dollars a month. This is just another way of adding to the bottom line of saving $1000 in 90 days.

Chapter 58

Day 58 CHALLENGE

God bless you and good evening. Welcome to Day 58 of the **"Save $1000 in 90-Days Challenge."** Are you ready for your fifty eighth day of challenge to help you save $1000 in the next 90 Days?

TODAY'S WORD

DECISION. The word decision is defined as a conclusion or resolution reached after consideration. Most people never really make real decisions about their finances. They simply live a life of hoping and wishing for things to change but the change they're hoping and wishing for does not come. You must come to a conclusion and resolution about your finances, don't just sit back and wait and do nothing, do something. If that something is only acquiring knowledge about how to improve your finances and then apply the knowledge that you learn. Don't sit back and just wait for money, just waiting dis-empowers you, taking actions empowers you. Make a decision to do something and you will find out that the money will show up. God responds to action not inaction and faith without works is DEAD!

DAY 58 CHALLENGE

Come to a decision about something that will increase your finances.

Many of you have been sitting by idly waiting for something to happen. Well if you don't do nothing, nothing from nothing leaves nothing. People that succeed financially are doers not hopers or wishers. Make a decision to do what you've been putting off, do it now! Some of you are waiting for a voice from heaven to tell you every little action to take, well in that case you don't need a brain to decide, why did God give us brains? To think, to decide, to do. If you acknowledge him he will direct your path, but even with that you have to come to a decision to acknowledge him.

If you're going wrong ask God to redirect you and if he doesn't at various points then just keep going until he redirects you.

Chapter 59

Day 59 CHALLENGE

God bless you and good evening. Welcome to Day 59 of the **"Save $1000 in 90-Days Challenge."** Are you ready for your fifty ninth day of challenge to help you save $1000 in the next 90 Days?

TODAY'S WORD

NETWORK. Network is defined as having a supportive system of sharing information and services among individuals and groups having a common interest. Do you have a network of people that you have a common interest with? Individuals with whom you can get together with to share your ideas, concepts or business plans with? If not you should because you never know who may be able to assist you in your endeavors.

DAY 59 CHALLENGE

Use the name of Jesus for the remaining 31 days.

Save $1000 In 90 Days Challenge

My Pastor taught a word about the name of Jesus. Saying there is power in the name of Jesus and that name can change your circumstances and situations. That name will work for your finances when you use it appropriately. Especially as a Christian you have the legal right and authority to use that name to give you the advantage in life. Say the name for your financial situation to help you save $1000 in 90 days. That name works in both the visible and the invisible realm. The word of God say *"Whatsoever ye shall ask (this word ask means to demand and command, your situation and circumstances to change) in my name, that will I do, that the Father may be glorified in the Son." John 14:13* For the remaining 31 days use the mighty and powerful name of JESUS!

Chapter 60

Day 60 CHALLENGE

God bless you and good evening. Welcome to Day 60 of the **"Save $1000 in 90-Days Challenge."** Are you ready for your sixty day of challenge to help you save $1000 in the next 90 Days?

TODAY'S WORD

COUNTDOWN. As we come to the last 30 days of the challenge there is still time to fulfill the challenge of saving $1000 in 90 days. The pressure is on and you're the right person for the task. You chose to be a part of this assignment because you wanted to change the financial course of your life. Thirty days is still enough time and the countdown is on, don't give up now for your will reap if you faint not.

DAY 60 CHALLENGE

Go through your house and sell all things you no longer need.

Save $1000 In 90 Days Challenge

Here is a way to put a lot of money in your Prosperity Bank in a short period of time. Start cleaning and sell everything that you haven't used this year. If you haven't used it in a year how much need do you really have for it? Sell it at a flea market, yard sale, on ebay, craigslist, etc... Use any online or offline place you can think of. JUST SELL EVERYTHING YOU REALLY DON'T NEED! It's money in your account.

Chapter 61

Day 61 CHALLENGE

God bless you and good evening. Welcome to Day 61 of the **"Save $1000 in 90-Days Challenge."** Are you ready for your sixty first of challenge to help you save $1000 in the next 90 Days?

TODAY'S WORD

MULTIPLE STREAMS OF INCOME. In order to always be on top of your financial situation why not have more than one stream of income coming in. When you have only one stream and it dries up through, loss of job, downsizing, business failure etc... Then your only resource of income is now gone. What will you do?

In order to not put yourself in such a dire situation you need to have multiple (many, several) streams of income. If one resource dries up then you still have other streams of income still coming in.

DAY 61 CHALLENGE

Create another stream of income.

What you need to understand with this is that there is always another way to make money. Creating another stream of income will give you another resource of financial flow. Another stream of income will give you the opportunity to make things happen and not just sit around waiting on one method of payment for your income. Also, the more income streams you have the more money you can bank and store up for any emergencies that may arise. Start that income stream today!

CHAPTER 62

Day 62 CHALLENGE

God bless you and good evening. Welcome to Day 62 of the **"Save $1000 in 90-Days Challenge."** Are you ready for your sixty second day of challenge to help you save $1000 in the next 90 Days?

TODAY'S WORD

THOUSANDAIRE. You have heard of the term MILLIONAIRE and one definition of a millionaire is a person whose wealth amounts to a million or more in some unit of currency or assets. Well a THOUSANDAIRE is a person whose wealth amounts to a thousand or more in some unit of currency or assets. Many people want to be a millionaire but they have not become a thousandaire yet? The goal of the 90 day challenge is to get a thousand dollars or more in your possession and we have 28 days left for you to fulfill that goal. Some of the challenges that we've written on in the past if you haven't done them go back and see which ones you're able to do in these remaining days. Your financial situation will change if you're willing to make the changes to change your situation.

DAY 62 CHALLENGE

Go back and check out some of the challenges that you haven't done yet and do them.

Chapter 63

Day 63 CHALLENGE

God bless you and good evening. Welcome to Day 63 of the **"Save $1000 in 90-Days Challenge."** Are you ready for your sixty third day of challenge to help you save $1000 in the next 90 Days?

TODAY'S WORD

GIVE. Giving is always a truth that is relevant in any time. As we celebrate the resurrection of Jesus Christ, the word of God tells us that "God so loved the world, that he gave his only Son, that whoever believes in him should not perish but have everlasting life." John 3:16 Since the Creator of all mankind GAVE shouldn't we also be givers. Because he gave his one Son today he has many sons. Hebrews 2:12

DAY 63 CHALLENGE

Become a giver.

For the remaining 27 days become a giver. Let the idea of giving consume you and whatever you give you shall receive in return. Give someone money and you will receive money back. Give what you give from the heart and God will see to it that you will receive kind in like manner. The word of God says, *"Give, and it shall be given unto you; good measure, pressed down, and shaken together, and running over, shall men give into your bosom. For with the same measure that ye mete withal it shall be measured to you again."* *Luke 6:38* When you give to the poor you are actually giving to God. *"He that hath pity upon the poor lendeth unto the Lord; and that which he hath given will he pay him again."* *Proverbs 19:17*

Chapter 64

Day 64 CHALLENGE

God bless you and good evening. Welcome to Day 64 of the **"Save $1000 in 90-Days Challenge."** Are you ready for your sixty fourth day of challenge to help you save $1000 in the next 90 Days?

TODAY'S WORD

FLEXIBILITY. Among the many traits that are shared by people that creates their destiny, one of the main ones are FLEXIBILITY. Flexibility is defined as: being ready, willing and able to move in a direction that you were not originally intending to go. Flexibility is the difference between taking the initiative to do something even though it bends you somewhat in another direction. Are you willing to turn and do something that can help you get to the $1000 you need when an opportunity presents itself? If you are then you're flexible, if you're not then you're inflexible, fixed, unbudgeable and unchangeable.

DAY 64 CHALLENGE

Use your skills as a house cleaner or organizer.

Are you good at house cleaning or organizing things? Why not start you a side gig and help others clean their house or organize it. You can begin to do this by offering a weekly housecleaning service or just charge a onetime fee for a large job. You can also help others organize their closets, attics or garages and charge a flat fee. You can even clean houses by contracting your work to Real Estate companies to clean homes when others move out to get it ready for the new occupants.

Chapter 65

Day 65 CHALLENGE

God bless you and good evening. Welcome to Day 65 of the **"Save $1000 in 90-Days Challenge."** Are you ready for your sixty fifth day of challenge to help you save $1000 in the next 90 Days?

TODAY'S WORD

UTILIZE. The word utilize is defined as: to put to use; turn to profitable account. Many times people are looking for something outside of themselves but all they need is already within their possession or person. If you will use what you already have more will be given you.

DAY 65 CHALLENGE

If you have dollars in your possession take and put them in your prosperity bank.

If you can't put all of them at least put some of

them into your Prosperity Bank, this will only add to your bottom line and help you to reach your goal of saving $1000 in 90 days.

Chapter 66

Day 66 CHALLENGE

God bless you and good evening. Welcome to Day 66 of the **"Save $1000 in 90-Days Challenge."** Are you ready for your sixty sixth day of challenge to help you save $1000 in the next 90 Days?

TODAY'S WORD

F.O.C.U.S. This is an acronym for Financial Organization Creates Unlimited Success.

DAY 66 CHALLENGE

Choose a system to start organizing your finances.

There are many ways to organize your finances, for some the best way is to use a program like Quicken for others it may be simply using pencil and paper. Without a system of some sort your financial life will continue to drift and increase will evade you at every turn. Being organized is essential to efficient money management. START ORGAN-

IZING YOUR FINANCES TODAY!

Chapter 67

Day 67 CHALLENGE

God bless you and good evening. Welcome to Day 67 of the **"Save $1000 in 90-Days Challenge."** Are you ready for your sixty seventh day of challenge to help you save $1000 in the next 90 Days?

TODAY'S WORD

STAY ON COURSE. It's so easy to get off of course when you're striving to achieve a goal. From day 1 your goal has been to save $1000 in 90 days, you may have gotten side tracked along the way but the race is not given to the swift but to them that endure to the end.

DAY 67 CHALLENGE

Skip the movies and make it a Netflix night.

This is another way to save money and add to your bottom line. Make this sacrifice this week and put that money in your Prosperity Bank. With the cost of a movie around $8.00 or more, popcorn and soda another $7.00, that's $15. That may not sound like much but it adds to the bottom line and help you to stay on course to reach your goal of saving $1000 in 90 days.

Chapter 68

Day 68 CHALLENGE

God bless you and good evening. Welcome to Day 68 of the **"Save $1000 in 90-Days Challenge."** Are you ready for your sixty eighth day of challenge to help you save $1000 in the next 90 Days?

TODAY'S WORD

FORWARD MARCH. You are 68 days into the challenge and your consistency has gotten you this far. Look at your Prosperity Bank, when you started 68 days ago you did not have that. But today you are going forward and there's no stopping you now. Forward march toward your $1000 saved in 90 days.

DAY 68 CHALLENGE

Put all the change you accumulate from today and the entire weekend into your prosperity bank.

Doing this will add to the bottom line and increase your Prosperity Bank that much more.

Chapter 69

Day 69 CHALLENGE

God bless you and good evening. Welcome to Day 69 of the **"Save $1000 in 90-Days Challenge."** Are you ready for your sixty ninth day of challenge to help you save $1000 in the next 90 Days?

TODAY'S WORD

MAGNETIZE. What you focus on is drawn to you, whether it is:

- Poverty or Plenty
- Barely Making ends Meet or Abundance
- Lack or Luxury

What you focus on you will attract and there is no way around it. You will magnetize the dominating thoughts of your mind. So let your thoughts be thoughts of increase, prosperity, save $1000 in 90 days and unlimited wealth. *For as a man thinketh in his heart so is he.*

DAY 69 CHALLENGE

Think only prosperous thoughts of increase and savings for the remaining 21 days.

For what you think you will soon become.

Chapter 70

Day 70 CHALLENGE

God bless you and good evening. Welcome to Day 70 of the **"Save $1000 in 90-Days Challenge."** Are you ready for your seventy day of challenge to help you save $1000 in the next 90 Days?

TODAY'S WORD

EVENT. If you allow it this 90 day challenge can be a turning point in your life financially. An event is a thing that happens, especially one of importance. An event can change your life for the better if you're willing to allow that event to modify your thinking and your actions. New thoughts and new actions will produce new results.

DAY 70 CHALLENGE

Stop using ATM's outside of your bank.

When you refuse to use ATM'S other than your bank you will save about $2-$3 per transaction.

Save $1000 In 90 Days Challenge

If you us an ATM twice a week that can add up to $4-$6 a week and $16 to $24 a month. Take this extra cash and put it in your Prosperity Bank. Even though it may be handy and convenient it's taking away not adding to your bottom line. A dollar saved is a dollar earned.

Chapter 71

Day 71 CHALLENGE

God bless you and good evening. Welcome to Day 71 of the **"Save $1000 in 90-Days Challenge."** Are you ready for your seventy first day of challenge to help you save $1000 in the next 90 Days?

TODAY'S WORD

BECOME A MAGNET TO MONEY. When you learn how to become a magnet to money then you want have to chase after money, because money will love to be in your possession. Most people don't attract money they repel money.

DAY 71 CHALLENGE

*Begin to say throughout the day "I **am a magnet to money."***

Chapter 72

Day 72 CHALLENGE

God bless you and good evening. Welcome to Day 72 of the **"Save $1000 in 90-Days Challenge."** Are you ready for your seventy second day of challenge to help you save $1000 in the next 90 Days?

TODAY'S WORD

HOW ARE YOU FEELING? Your feelings have a lot to do with what you accomplish in life. Notice when you are negative you feel down but when you're positive you feel up. Your feeling send forth a release of energy that attracts to you according to how you feel. Feel increase, prosperity and wealth and you will begin to attract these things in your life.

DAY 72 CHALLENGE

Put the biggest bill you can afford in your prosperity bank.

If you don't have any bills today make sure

you do it by the weekend, this will only add to the bottom line, money in your Prosperity Bank.

Chapter 73

Day 73 CHALLENGE

God bless you and good evening. Welcome to Day 73 of the **"Save $1000 in 90-Days Challenge."** Are you ready for your seventy third day of challenge to help you save $1000 in the next 90 Days?

TODAY'S WORD

INSANITY. One definition of insanity is to keep doing the same things but expect different results. The dictionary defines insanity as the state of being seriously mentally ill; madness, extreme foolishness or irrationality. If you want a financial change in your life but you're doing the same things you've been doing for years; you are experiencing madness, serious mental illness and extreme foolishness.

DAY 73 CHALLENGE

Avoid whole life insurance and buy term and save the difference.

Save $1000 In 90 Days Challenge

Whole life policies are expensive for the policy owner and lucrative for the policy seller. Term policies, which cover you for a set period, are FAR less expensive.

Chapter 74

Day 74 CHALLENGE

God bless you and good evening. Welcome to Day 74 of the **"Save $1000 in 90-Days Challenge."** Are you ready for your seventy fourth day of challenge to help you save $1000 in the next 90 Days?

TODAY'S WORD

IT IS GOD THAT GIVETH THEE POWER TO GET WEALTH. This is a scripture from Deuteronomy 8:18 and the scripture states that it is God that gives you the power (ability) to get wealth. If God has already given you the ability to get wealth then why don't you have it? The reason that people are not further financially is because they don't have the proper knowledge.

DAY 74 CHALLENGE

Read Deuteronomy 8:18 & Deuteronomy 28.

The word of God is lamp unto our feet, and a

light unto our paths. Psalms 119:105 When we come to the knowledge that the word of God truly has the answers to all of life situations and circumstances then we are not far from the kingdom of God. Mark 12:34

Chapter 75

Day 75 CHALLENGE

God bless you and good evening. Welcome to Day 75 of the **"Save $1000 in 90-Days Challenge."** Are you ready for your seventy fifth day of challenge to help you save $1000 in the next 90 Days?

TODAY'S WORD

TEST. The only way that you will be, have and do more is you will have to pass the tests of life. God will not just hand over financial prosperity or wealth to you until you have showed that you're able to handle the small amounts that you have to manage. A test is defined as: a procedure intended to establish the quality, performance, or reliability of something, especially before it is taken into widespread use.

CHALLENGE FOR TODAY

Become a freelancer.

Save $1000 In 90 Days Challenge

You're good at something, God gave you a gift and a talent and somebody wants to pay you to do what you do best.

- What are you good at?
- What does others rave about that you do?
- What do you do with ease?
- Can you teach somebody to do that?
- Can you do that for somebody(s)?

Become a freelancer and get paid for what you do best and then save what you make in your Prosperity Bank. Adding always to the bottom line of saving $1000 in 90 days!

Chapter 76

Day 76 CHALLENGE

God bless you and good evening. Welcome to day 76 of the **"Save $1000 in 90 Day Challenge."** Are you ready for day seventy sixth of challenge?

Today's Word

MONEY. The money that you need, desire or want is in the hands of somebody else. The word of God says *"Men shall give unto your bosom."* Luke 6:38

DAY 76 CHALLENGE

Take $10 and put it in your prosperity bank.

Instead of spending that extra money on something that you can do without add it somewhere that it will truly count. It's all adding to your bottom line.

If you don't have it today make sure that you add this amount as soon as you can.

Chapter 77

Day 77 CHALLENGE

God bless you and good evening. Welcome to Day 77 of the **"Save $1000 in 90-Days Challenge."** Are you ready for your seventy seventh day of challenge to help you save $1000 in the next 90 Days?

TODAY'S WORD

IS MONEY SPIRITUAL? Don't get so spiritual that you think money is non-spiritual. God is a Spirit and He said that *"Money Answers All Things." Ecc. 10:19* If anyone knows that money has a spiritual undertone it's God himself. He even places great emphasis on money, even telling us to bring the tithes into his house. *Malachi 3:10*

DAY 77 CHALLENGE

Pay your bills on time.

When you pay your bills on time then you want have to worry about late fees, credit card interest and penalties that can really add up. Begin to pay your bills on time and the late fees that you use to payout, put them into your Prosperity Bank.

Chapter 78

Day 78 CHALLENGE

God bless you and good evening. Welcome to Day 78 of the **"Save $1000 in 90-Days Challenge."** Are you ready for your seventy eighth day of challenge to help you save $1000 in the next 90 Days?

TODAY'S WORD

FIND YOUR PASSION. If you were to win $10 million dollars on tomorrow would you keep working your job or business or would you quit it and do something else? Give an honest answer.

If you would do something else then you're not currently doing your passion. No amount of money will cause you to leave your passion; money will only equip you to be able to do more of your passion.

DAY 78 CHALLENGE

Find your passion-do your passion-and the money

will come.

Not only will saving a $1000 be an easy financial task but you will be able to fulfill many financial goals because you will be doing what you love. 95% of people are doing something other than what they love; they are doing it solely for the money, yet dreading to go to work every day. If you feel like this then you're far away from your PASSION! FIND YOUR PASSION-DO YOUR PASSION-AND THE MONEY WILL COME!

Chapter 79

Day 79 CHALLENGE

God bless you and good evening. Welcome to Day 79 of the **"Save $1000 in 90-Days Challenge."** Are you ready for your seventy ninth day of challenge to help you save $1000 in the next 90 Days?

TODAY'S WORD

DESTINATION. Do you know where you are going financially? A destination is defined as: the place to which someone or something is going. If you don't know where you're going any place will get you there. Make your destination sure and you will arrive at the place you were meant to be, A PLACE OF INCREASE & PROSPERITY!

DAY 79 CHALLENGE

Consider shopping online for items.

When you shop online for items you can save money in several ways.

1. Look for and ask about FREE SHIPPING.
2. Search for a coupon code.
3. Look for sites that will give you cash back for ordering.

The money that you will save by buying online put it in your Prosperity Bank. The difference in the FREE SHIPPING, COUPON CODE AND CASH BACK. It all adds to the bottom line, money to help you reach your goal of saving $1000 in 90 days.

Chapter 80

Day 80 CHALLENGE

God bless you and good evening. Welcome to Day 80 of the **"Save $1000 in 90-Days Challenge."** Are you ready for your eighth day of challenge to help you save $1000 in the next 90 Days?

TODAY'S WORD

ACCELERATION. We are now at day 80 of our 90 day challenge to save $1000 in 90 days. WOW! We have 10 days left to meet our goal or get as close to it as possible. The word acceleration means to increase in the rate or speed of something. In this case you need to increase the rate or speed of your saving in order to reach your goal. You've come a long ways and in these last 10 days you need to accelerate your savings at a greater velocity of speed.

DAY 80 CHALLENGE

Get your money.

Save $1000 In 90 Days Challenge

Go forth and get the rest of your money that you need to fulfill your goal. For eighty days you have heard how to save and make money to reach your $1000 challenge, some of these challenges could have put hundreds of dollars in your pocket at one time, go back and check through them to see which one you can implement and put into action immediately.

Chapter 81

Day 81 CHALLENGE

God bless you and good evening. Welcome to Day 81 of the **"Save $1000 in 90-Days Challenge."** Are you ready for your eighty first day of challenge to help you save $1000 in the next 90 Days?

TODAY'S WORD

BURNING DESIRE. One thing you must have to achieve your goal of saving $1000 in 90 days, it's not money and it's not intelligence-- it's a burning desire to save that $1000 in 90 days.

CHALLENGE FOR TODAY

Take the largest bill that you can afford and put it in your prosperity bank now.

If you don't have the bill today then make a vow to yourself that you will do it before the week is out. No matter what else you have to do, DO THIS! The person with a desire will just read this and say it's a good idea but the person with a BURNING DESIRE will do whatever they have to do to make it happen. Do you have a desire or a burning desire?

Chapter 82

Day 82 CHALLENGE

God bless you and good evening. Welcome to Day 82 of the **"Save $1000 in 90-Days Challenge."** Are you ready for your eighty second day of challenge to help you save $1000 in the next 90 Days?

TODAY'S WORD

FINANCIAL PROSPERITY IS OF THE SPIRIT. The answers to all your prosperity questions such as; how to acquire more finances, where they are, how to make money work for you and how to continually reach your financial goals are within your spirit for it's in your spirit that the Spirit of God resides.

DAY 82 CHALLENGE

Get along with your spirit and ask the Lord all your prosperity questions.

You need to ask God to give you the wisdom that you need to prosper financially. Financial increase and prosperity is of the spirit and when you can get both your spirit and mind working in complete harmony you will never again dwell another day in lack, poverty, barely making ends meet or paycheck living. Ask the Holy Spirit questions about financial increase He knows all "*for the Spirit searcheth all things, yea, the deep things of God. 1 Corinthians 2:10*

Chapter 83

Day 83 CHALLENGE

God bless you and good evening. Welcome to Day 83 of the **"Save $1000 in 90-Days Challenge."** Are you ready for your eighty third day of challenge to help you save $1000 in the next 90 Days?

TODAY'S WORD

THE BEST IS YET TO COME. We have one week left for the conclusion of the Save $1000 in 90 Days Challenge. WOW! My question to you is how was the CHALLENGE? Did it challenge you to think outside the box? Were many of these challenges new to you?

With one week left I would like to hear your feedback.

- Are you on target to reach your goal?
- What did you learn from the challenge?
- Do you have a new mindset for saving?
- Will you continue it for another 90 days?
- Were the challenges difficult?

Only seven days left, let's make the best of it and add more to the bottom line in these remaining 7 days.

DAY 83 CHALLENGE

Take the time to meditate on the challenges.

Take some time to meditate on what God has blessed you to accomplish financially these 83 days if you have followed the challenges. Meditation is an awesome spiritual principle that will guarantee you success in any area of life. In Joshua 1:8 it says, *"This book of the law shall not depart out of thy mouth; but thy shalt MEDITATE therein day and night, then thou shalt make thy way PROSPEROUS, and then thou shalt have good SUCCESS."*

1. Think about the money that you have accumulated that you did not have before.

2. Think about how you put that money in your Prosperity Jar consistently.

3. Think about the sacrifices you made to

reach, come close to or even just have saved a couple extra hundred dollars that you did not have before.

This is the beginning of something great and it began with YOU!

You can also email me your comments at: dljfc@yahoo.com

Chapter 84

Day 84 CHALLENGE

God bless you and good evening. Welcome to Day 84 of the **"Save $1000 in 90-Days Challenge."** Are you ready for your eighty fourth day of challenge to help you save $1000 in the next 90 Days?

TODAY'S WORD

REWARD. The Bible states *"that the race is not to the swift, nor the battle to the strong, neither yet bread to the wise, nor yet riches to men of understanding, nor yet favour to men of skill; but time and chance happeneth to them all."* Ecclesiastes 9:11 When your time and chance come the only way you will be rewarded is if you will see the job all the way through to the end.

DAY 84 CHALLENGE

Dedicate yourself to a certain amount that you will include in your prosperity bank in the closing 6 days of the challenge.

Save $1000 In 90 Days Challenge

My closing amount for this week will be $100 in my Prosperity Bank. What will yours be?

Chapter 85

Day 85 CHALLENGE

God bless you and good evening. Welcome to Day 85 of the **"Save $1000 in 90-Days Challenge."** Are you ready for your eighty fifth day of challenge to help you save $1000 in the next 90 Days?

TODAY'S WORD

WINNER. You are a winner and you have proved it by your consistent effort to accomplish this 90 day challenge. You have been attentive and persistent in your pursuit and your Prosperity Bank shows your efforts. Congratulation on 85 days of saving and managing your money.

DAY 85 CHALLENGE

Use coupons and then save the money you saved.

Many times when individuals save money from grocery shopping as a result of their coupon use they fail to save what they saved. You can save a tremendous amount of money using coupons. Some stores have double coupon days and you easily walk out with $100 worth of groceries for $25, $30, $35 etc… the bottom line is you have saved as a result of using coupons.

Now here is where most coupons users fail, they fail to put aside the money they just saved into a savings. If you got $100 worth of groceries for $30 then you should have put $70 into your Prosperity Bank. Using this method it is a win-win situation, you received the groceries at a discount price and you put the money you would have spent in your savings. WOW!

Chapter 86

Day 86 CHALLENGE

God bless you and good evening. Welcome to Day 86 of the **"Save $1000 in 90-Days Challenge."** Are you ready for your eighty sixth day of challenge to help you save $1000 in the next 90 Days?

TODAY'S WORD

MISSION. Only the individuals that see the challenge more than just something to do but a true mission to fulfill will actually fulfill this important assignment carried out for financial purposes.

DAY 86 CHALLENGE

Take out the largest bill that you can afford and put it in your prosperity bank.

As we come to a close of the 90 Days Challenge everything that you put in your Prosperity Bank is simply adding to the bottom line. Four days to go and what a journey.

Chapter 87

Day 87 CHALLENGE

God bless you and good evening. Welcome to Day 87 of the **"Save $1000 in 90-Days Challenge."** Are you ready for your eighty seventh day of challenge to help you save $1000 in the next 90 Days?

TODAY'S WORD

CIRCUMSTANCES. Circumstances do not make the person but a person makes their circumstances. Where you are at the moment is not as important as where you're going and when you change your thoughts and actions then your circumstances will change automatic.

CHALLENGE FOR TODAY

Take time to be grateful for this 90 day challenge journey.

Being grateful is a treasure within itself because when you're grateful it attracts to you even more blessings.

Chapter 88

Day 88 CHALLENGE

God bless you and good evening. Welcome to Day 88 of the **"Save $1000 in 90-Days Challenge."** Are you ready for your eighty eighth day of challenge to help you save $1000 in the next 90 Days?

TODAY'S WORD

ANSWERS. When you have **answers** then you have solutions to problems and when you have solutions then you're able to meet needs.

DAY 88 CHALLENGE

Get a roll of quarters and add it to your prosperity bank.

If you don't have it today then get it by the end of the week to add to the bottom line of saving $1000 in 90 days.

Chapter 89

Day 89 CHALLENGE

God bless you and good evening. Welcome to Day 89 of the **"Save $1000 in 90-Days Challenge."** Are you ready for your eighty ninth day of challenge to help you save $1000 in the next 90 Days?

TODAY'S WORD

BLUEPRINT. A blueprint is like a design plan that shows you what to do and how to do it. For the past 88 days you've had a daily plan that showed you how to save and make $1000 in 90 days. If you've followed the plan you should be rejoicing right about now because you have either reached your $1000 goal or you have saved a considerable amount that's more than you had 88 days ago.

DAY 89 CHALLENGE

Convert setbacks into opportunities.

Whatever you didn't accomplish these 90 days

don't see it as a setback but as an opportunity to learn from your mistakes. Learn what you can do that you didn't do and do it in the next 90 day challenge.

Chapter 90

Day 90 CHALLENGE

God bless you and good evening. We have come to the conclusion of the **"Save $1000 in 90 Days Challenge."**

TODAY'S WORD

FINISHED TO START AGAIN. We have finally arrived at the 90th day of the Save $1000 in 90 days challenge. What a journey this has been, you have just finished up 90 straight days of saving and making money.

What do you think? What did you save? How was your journey? What did you learn? Well I tell you this was truly an amazing experience of discipline and focus; I will never be the same when it comes to saving and making money. I am forever branded and committed to saving money.

I want to thank you for taking the time to read these daily challenges and I pray that they were inspiring, enlightening and empowering for you financially. Your life both mentally and financially will never be the same. Once the mind has been stretched it can never go back to its original state

Congratulations on finishing this challenge but don't let it be an end, to continue saving just start over just as if it was day 1 and begin the whole process again. Do you know what happens when you begin the process again? You will save another $1000 and continue to add to your bottom line. You can go back through the process again by simply starting back at the beginning at day 1 and continue for the next 90 days.

Do you know that most individuals never finish anything? That's why New Year's resolutions are mostly a waste of time because after about 2 -3 weeks' individuals have retreated back to their old self. You finished this challenge and have made a mark in your life that can never be erased. WOW! That's not an easy task and whether you saved $1000 or $300 you are further than you were before you started. Keep doing the same thing and you will get the same results, more savings and forever adding to the bottom line.

If you're ready to go further than just saving a $1000 and ready start to eliminating your debts then join us for the next financial phase of your life. Otherwise, just continue the Save $1000 challenge for those that want to go at it once again. Thank you very much for your participation and time and remember:

"If You Want the Things in Your Life to Change Then You Must Change the Things in Your Life."

Note:

To go to the next phase of your financial life, go to our website at: www.dexterljones.com to learn how to save $15,000 in 365 days.